Death, and the Day's Light

Endowed by
TOM WATSON BROWN
and
THE WATSON-BROWN FOUNDATION, INC.

Death, and the Day's Light

Poems

James Dickey

Edited with Commentary by Gordon Van Ness

MERCER UNIVERSITY PRESS | *Macon, Georgia*

MUP/ H899

© 2015 James Dickey Estate
Published by Mercer University Press
1501 Mercer University Drive
Macon, Georgia 31207
All rights reserved

9 8 7 6 5 4 3 2 1

Books published by Mercer University Press are printed on acid-free paper that meets the requirements of the American National Standard for Information Sciences—Permanence of Paper for Printed Library Materials.

ISBN   978-0-88146-519-8
Cataloging-in-Publication Data is available from the
Library of Congress

For my wife Dawn,
>   who brings the light,

>   and

For my children—Dylan, Brooke Elizabeth, Ian, Gordon, and Courteney,
>   who show the way

>   Who has told you what discoveries
>   There are, along the stressed blank
>   Of a median line? From it, nothing

>   Can finally fall. Like a spellbinder's pass
>   A tense placid principle continues

>   Over it, and when you follow you have the drift,

>   The balance of many compass needles
> Verging to the pole.

>   James Dickey, "Basics"

Contents

Foreword, *by Christopher Dickey*	ix
Acknowledgments	xii
Commentary, *by Gordon Van Ness*	xiv
Editorial Note	xxxiii
Photographs	xxxix
Death, and the Day's Light	1
Two Poems: Son and His Mother	1
Conch	3
The Drift-Spell	5
Last Hours	7
The Confederate Line at Ogeechee Creek	13
Entering Scott's Night	14
Two Poems on the Survival of the Male Body	17
Show Us the Sea	19
For Jules Bacon	53
Afterword, *by Dave Smith*	79
Index	89

Foreword

By Christopher Dickey

When my father, who was dying, asked me to bring him a voluminous pile of papers from the dining room table, I wasn't sure what he had in mind.

"They say 'Show Us the Sea,'" he said.

"Sure," I said. A poem, I thought. But it took me a minute to find it. Almost every flat surface in the house was stacked with books and drafts of poems, pages of essays, random thoughts, drafted letters or bits and pieces of his latest novel.

My father, seventy-three years old and terribly frail because of the fibrosis consuming his lungs, sat in an old corduroy-covered armchair like an aging monarch on a battered throne, surveying a kingdom of the mind. Around him books rose in erratic columns – books by poets, books of criticism, books that explored the lives and sensibilities of other artists, including filmmakers and painters.

When students, friends or admirers, some of whom were complete strangers, showed up at the door, he would invite them in to talk, and inevitably he would ask them to search out some particular volume from the thousands on our shelves so he could read them a passage, or have them read it to him. Inevitably those books remained by his chair. And the columns grew. On one of them he posed, precariously, a large glass of chocolate milk. Nearby, an oxygen generator purred and chugged, feeding breath to him through the tube beneath his nose.

"Here it is," I called out to him.

"Bring it to me, Chrissy," he said. (I was forty-five at the time, but nicknames know no age.)

We looked at the first pages, annotated heavily with my father's angular script. "Last Draft," he had written at the top, then typed in capital letters, "TWO POEMS ON THE SURVIVAL OF THE MALE BODY." More notes suggested he was pondering epigraphs by the English poet Thomas Lovell Beddoes and the German Friedrich Hölderlin. Then came the beginning of the first of those two poems of survival, "Show us the Sea": "Real God, roll," it read, with two arrows drawn in suggesting those words might be moved to the right on the page or might be moved down.

My father said, with a touch of ironic humor and a kind of resignation, that he had worked on these poems for years, and that he thought they were the most important poems he had written. Certainly they were very important to him at that moment. And he asked me to finish them for him after he died.

"I could try," I said, "but *you* will finish them." I was anxious to turn the conversation away from death, and certain that if ever I did try to take these sprawling poems in hand, I could not find the right voice. I am a writer, but not a poet, nor a scholar of my father's work.

A few months later, after my father's death had come, I did call up a draft of those poems on my computer screen and page through, and I tried to begin to edit, or re-compose them. But my lines on the survival of the male body were stillborn. I closed the file, and did not reopen it.

Years passed.

More than a decade after my father's death, Gordon Van Ness got in touch with me with a surprising proposition. He said he would like to try to finish the two poems, to the extent possible, from the many manuscript versions stored at Emory University. Gordon is one of the best, most conscientious scholars to have studied my father's work. He had edited the definitive two-volume collection of his correspondence, *The One Voice of James Dickey,* and I knew that if anyone could find the true voice in those poems, he could. I asked my brother Kevin, whose image is central to the first poem, and my sister Bronwen, who has a wonderful literary sensibility, if they would agree to grant permission. They did. And then the work began.

I don't think any of us anticipated what a labor of diligence, doubts, creativity, and frustrations this turned out to be. I do think there must have been times when Gordon wanted to walk away from the whole project. But he did not. It had become, unquestionably, a labor of love. And what Gordon has done with those two poems is truly remarkable: he has found the voice of James Dickey; he has resurrected the genius.

More, even than that, in this book, *Death, and the Day's Light,* Gordon has put those two poems in a context that is as honest as it is enlightening for readers who are not yet familiar with James Dickey's work: the poetry and the criticism as well as *Deliverance* and the other novels. There is no glossing over the fact that for many years, as my father tried to write through a fog of alcohol, some of his oeuvre suffered. In the magnificent edition of *The Complete Poems of James Dickey*, edited by Ward Briggs, you can read the great, the good, and the really-not-very-good-at-all poetry that he produced in his long career. But in the mid-1990s, in those years when my father was slowly dying, but no longer drinking, his poetry took on new life and a new, more disciplined intensity that is reflected in the other poems Gordon has included in this collection.

This, James Dickey's final volume of poems, beautifully produced by Marc Jolley and his team at Mercer University Press, is also one of his most intriguing. Written at the end of his life, it brings us back to the beginnings. He has shown us his amazing sensibility. He has shown us the sea. He has survived.

Christopher Dickey

Acknowledgments

Clichés of acknowledgment are sometimes accurate. *Death, and the Day's Light*, the final volume of poems on which Dickey was working when he died, simply would not have been possible without the assistance and generosity of many people.

    I am grateful for the unwavering support of the Dickey Estate, in particular Christopher Dickey, but also Kevin Dickey and Bronwen Dickey. They approved my request to edit their father's manuscript and consistently facilitated my efforts to publish it. Christopher wrote a foreword. All offered memories and facts as well as encouragement. So, too, did Deborah Dickey, whose recollection of the origins of "The Confederate Line at Ogeechee Creek" enhanced my knowledge of Dickey's creativity and the way he transformed experience. Judy Baughman was similarly helpful regarding the event sponsored by the University of South Carolina that inspired "Entering Scott's Night." Tim Guthrie graciously answered my many questions regarding Guthrie's lifeguarding and bodybuilding experiences on Pawleys Island and his conversations with Dickey. Carol Fairman and Meg Richards, Dickey's office assistants during the mid-1990s, provided me with an understanding of his work; they clarified my sense of the last years of Dickey's life and of the projects on which he labored.

    Of those who were or are in academe, I am especially grateful to Don Greiner, who steadfastly believed in the worthiness of this project. He read the edits and the commentary, facilitated by his infamous red pens, and in so doing improved the manuscript. Ernest Suarez offered needed counsel, and Henry Hart answered my queries, enabling me among other things to locate and interview Mrs. Earl Bradley, wife of Dickey's pilot during World War II, who shared information regarding camp life and her deceased husband's relationship with Dickey. Ward Briggs' own research enabled me to work knowledgeably. Joyce Pair generously shared photographs of Dickey that she had taken over the years as founder and editor of the *James Dickey Newsletter*.

    Kathy Shoemaker of the Manuscript, Archives, and Rare Book Library of Emory University oversaw and coordinated my request for more than one thousand pages of Dickey papers. Wendell Barbour, director of Greenwood Library of Longwood University, provided the necessary funding to secure Dickey papers. Lisa Seamster offered computer and copying assistance when she could least afford the time.

Dave Smith graciously agreed to write an afterword for this volume. His critical acumen and poetic sensitivities command my utmost respect. After comparing the edits of "Show Us the Sea" and "For Jules Bacon" with the final drafts of these poems, he convinced me that I had captured Dickey's voice. David Bottoms was similarly supportive, reading the edits and encouraging me to seek publication.

Jonathan Haupt and the University of South Carolina Press generously granted permission to include the five short poems—"Conch," "The Drift-Spell," "Last Hours," "The Confederate Line at Ogeechee Creek," and "Entering Scott's Night"—published previously in Ward Briggs' fine volume *The Complete Poems of James Dickey*.

Finally, Marc Jolley at Mercer University Press deserves my deep gratitude for his enthusiastic willingness to publish *Death, and the Day's Light*. If Dickey's career is resurrected almost twenty years following his death, his desire to publish this collection will have been a large contributing factor.

Commentary

In 1996, as James Dickey struggled with his impending death and endeavored to overcome it, an effort that had always energized his imagination, he re-established his priorities. Recognizing that he would die from suffocation brought on by fibrosis of the lungs, he attempted to wring two poems, "Show Us the Sea" and "For Jules Bacon," from his earlier works and from his old self, not the drunken genius but the football player and weight lifter, the combat aviator and caring father. The transformation was, in all important ways, a resurrection.

A year earlier, responding to an interviewer who had asked what he was experimenting with in his poetry, Dickey declared, "I like to work close to the margins of what has been done, or what I have done, and try to push it out a little more. Get out there where nobody can help you, where there's not any precedent—that's the thing that appeals to me." Specifically, he stated, he was working on two long poems grouped under the title "Two Poems on the Survival of the Male Body." Despite the publication three years earlier of *The Whole Motion: Collected Poems, 1945-1992*, Dickey had begun work on a new volume of poetry.

It was to this manuscript, however, now enlarged, that Dickey referred when he answered a query on 26 June 1996 from the editors of *The Oxford Quarterly Review*, who were inquiring whether he would submit for publication any new poems he had finished. "I would be glad to do that," he responded, "when I have completed what I am now working on, a suite of poems called On the Survival of the Male Body." Dickey then asked, "Would you like to see a section of one of these, excerpted so that it would constitute, say, an independent poem? I might be able to do this: have done it, in fact, for the opening was printed a couple of years ago in the *Partisan Review*, over here." That fragment, "Show Us the Sea," published in the summer 1990 issue, constituted part of the opening section of a long poem of the same title. Additionally, in his notes Dickey had projected a series of what he called "Out-takes," more intricate explorations, as it were, of specific images in the two long poems, and he identified these short works: "Conch," "The Drift-Spell," "Pier Bowling Alley," "Hero," "Sand-Aging," and "Wave and Slack

Return." He suggested to the editors of *The Oxford Quarterly Review* a specific "out-take": "The section I have in mind concerns a bowling alley on a pier, if that is any inducement."

Yet, during summer and fall 1996 as he struggled with illness, Dickey outwardly seemed not to focus on poetry at all but rather on his fiction, specifically *Crux*, the sequel to his massive 1987 novel *Alnilam*, which centered on a father's search for his son amid an attempted takeover by cadets of an Army Air Force base, as well as on the filming of *To the White Sea*, his 1993 novel about an American aviator shot down over Tokyo as that city is about to be firebombed. Film rights had been bought by the Coen Brothers. Don Greiner and Ben Franklin, faculty colleagues at the University of South Carolina with whom he shared weekly "power lunches" during the eighties and nineties, do not remember Dickey's discussion of or work on poetry in 1995-96, nor do Carol Fairman and Meg Richards, his office assistants during the years from 1994 until 1997.

Yet Dickey was clearly continuing his poetic efforts. Two additional "out-takes," "The Drift-Spell" and "Conch," had been published, the former in *James Dickey at 70: A Tribute* (later reprinted first in the *Princeton University Library Chronicle* in spring 1994 and then in *Atlanta* magazine in August 1995) and the latter in the spring/summer 1996 issue of *Apostrophe* (later reprinted in the 13 July 1996 issue of *The New Yorker*). Moreover, his initial conception of two long poems grouped together had yielded to a re-visioning of the volume as "a suite of poems." The title would be slightly shortened, *On the Survival of the Male Body*, but the collection would include more poems similarly themed. Later that fall or early winter, Dickey further restructured the volume. He grouped the two long poems, "Show Us the Sea" and "For Jules Bacon," under the heading "Two Poems on the Survival of the Male Body"; "Conch" and "The Drift-Spell" were similarly yoked as "Two Poems: Son and His Mother," the sets to conclude and open the volume, respectively. Dickey now titled the collection as *Death, and the Day's Light*, a line from "Show Us the Sea" which he also included in "The Drift-Spell." A folder thus labeled and which contained other poems for the volume resides among his papers at the Manuscript, Archives, and Rare Book Library of Emory University.

Dickey's deteriorating health, however, precluded his finishing either "Show Us the Sea" or "For Jules Bacon" and thus the volume itself. In October 1994, as a consequence of his alcoholism, he had developed a severe case of hepatitis, which weakened Dickey, leaving him often confined to a wheelchair. In February 1996, his lungs began to fail, the result of fibrosis that had developed independently of the liver condition and which required the use of portable oxygen. While Dickey remained critically astute and formidable in conversation, he understood that he would not live long enough to finish the two lengthy poems. He asked his older son Christopher, who was the Paris bureau chief for *Newsweek*, to complete "Show Us the Sea" and "For Jules Bacon." "My father wanted me to 'finish' those poems which he had wrestled with for so long," Chris stated, "But that is probably not the direction in which my talents lie." Following Dickey's death in January 1997, the poems remained incomplete, housed among his papers. In May 2009 Gordon Van Ness proposed to the Estate that he edit both poems, compile the volume, and include commentary and an editorial note. On behalf of Kevin and Bronwen, Dickey's other son and daughter and who were co-executors with him, Christopher agreed.

Death, and the Day's Light is thus, literally, the "last motion," but thematically it both alludes to his previous poetic efforts and summarizes his life as death approached. Dickey had declared that the poems in his "early motion" emerged from what he called "A night-rhythm, something felt in pulse, not word," an anapestic meter that was nothing less than a "self-generating on-go that seems to have existed before any poem and to continue after any actual poem ends." While the meter and stanza form in *Death, and the Day's Light* in no way reflect Dickey's "early motion," which was heavily influenced by such modernist dicta as structured lyrics, learned allusions, witty figures of speech, and verbal ambiguity, the subjects themselves do and in this sense continue the thematic concerns that were always Dickey's primary interests: family, war, death, and love. Moreover, the poems echo, in their images and dramatic situations, earlier works.

Those concerns, which Dickey explicitly announced in *Into the Stone* (1960), arranged in the order in which these interests generally appeared in his correspondence home from service bases in the States and camps in the Pacific during World War II, broadened in subsequent volumes. For example, what had been the primary concern in the "Family" section of *Into the Stone*, an attention to relations between brothers or between father and child, became enlarged in *Drowning with Others* (1962), his subsequent collection, to include not only associations based on authority, as in "The Lifeguard," but also connections between man and animal, as in "Listening to Foxhounds" and "Fog Envelops the Animals," a larger sense of kinship as it were. Dickey extended the meanings of the volume's other untitled but corresponding sections as well, those representing "War," "Death, and Others," and "Love," respectively. In each of these, the strict denotative definition expanded to encompass a wider grasp of the possibilities inherent in the concerns. *Helmets* (1964), Dickey's third volume, was an attempt, as he noted in *Self-Interviews*, "to deepen some of the themes announced in *Into the Stone*, but mainly in *Drowning with Others*. The hunting theme took on a much greater importance, and I wanted to get back to the war theme in a way that had nothing to do with flying." In an endeavor to intensify those concerns already declared, Dickey decided to move, in his words, "Not toward a number of other lyric poems about the subjects I wanted to deal with, but rather toward an attempt, in William James's great phrase, to turn 'the cube of reality,' to show the same action from different sides as seen or imagined by one person." The three war poems, for example, are situated not in the second section of *Helmets*, as one might expect given Dickey's arrangement of subjects, but in the fourth part, that section which in previous collections constituted the "Love" poems. In these poems Dickey achieves an accommodation with his memories of war and his guilt for surviving by fully indentifying with those who have died, feelings characterized as love. Such intimacy is perhaps best exhibited in "The Driver," when the speaker dives underwater at the war's end to sit in a foundered landing craft sunk during the invasion of the island:

> Driving through the country of the drowned
> On a sealed, secret-keeping breath,
> Ten feet under water I am still,
> Getting used to the burning stare
> Of the wide-eyed dead after battle.

I saw, through the sensitive roof—
The uneasy lyrical skin that lies
Between death and life, trembling always—.

In effect, Dickey's narrators, what he labeled his "I-figures," more and more search for and achieve transcendence, if only momentarily, a re-integration with larger forces; and they commit themselves to speaking out about the experiences, to giving back by communicating the possibility of meaning to others. The speaker in "On the Coosawattee," for example, asserts, "I taste the fretted light fall / Through living needles to be here / Like a word I can feed on forever / Or believe like I have / Or want to conceive out of greenness"; and in "Drinking from a Helmet," the last poem in the collection, the speaker, having relived a dying soldier's last thought of his younger brother, decides to tell the latter "where I had stood, / What poured, what spilled, what swallowed: / And tell him I was the man."

Dickey's decision to categorize his poetry in terms of various "motions" remains problematic, however, for it presupposes a clear and clean delineation among what he termed his "early," "central," and "late" poems. Dickey himself seemed aware of this over-simplification, writing in the preface to *The Early Motion* (1981) that in this volume "can be seen and heard the later motion, and doubtless, when all the poems are done, the whole motion as well." While it is true, moreover, that the poems in *The Central Motion* (1983) are more focused, less a display of what Doug Keesey calls "the volatile interplay of styles" in Dickey's early poetic efforts, even this grouping presents decided variety and linguistic experimentation. One would never, for example, consider Dickey's "Pine," a poem that uses associational imagery to depict the speaker's efforts to identify with a tree through "successive apprehensions," with *The Zodiac*, a long narrative that portrays the attempts of a drunken Dutch poet to connect with the universe, "The perpetual Eden of space." Dickey included both works in a motion that he called "the centrality in my writing life." The motions, in other words, overlap. Yet that stated, a more puzzling observation presents itself. Dickey's "early motion" consists of his first three volumes—*Into the Stone, Drowning with Others*, and *Helmets*. *The Early Motion*, however, completely omits *Into the Stone*.

In *The Whole Motion*, Dickey included some, though not all, of *Into the Stone*—only 15 of the original 24 poems. Though such exclusion owed partly to Wesleyan University Press's concern over size (*Puella* was similarly truncated), more than marketing was at issue in the tendency to downplay *Into the Stone*. Rather, Dickey's omissions resulted from his deliberate efforts to distance himself from almost any poem that affirmed modernist dicta.

After *Buckdancer's Choice* (1965) won the National Book Award for poetry, Dickey's poems changed focus. His next volume, *The Eye-Beaters, Blood, Victory, Madness, Buckhead and Mercy* (1970), initiated his "central motion"; the poems were more socially conscious, less centered on self, and revealed a preoccupation with mortality. The titles of these new poems, for example, "Diabetes," "Mercy," "Venom," "Knock," and "Madness," reflect the loss of afflatus and affirmation characteristic of the early volumes. They posit only death and uncertainty, the individual confronting unstoppable forces. The narrator in "The Cancer Match" realizes "I don't have all the time / In the world, but I have all night. / I have space for me and my house, / And I have cancer and whisky." Forty-seven years old in 1970, Dickey worried about his health. Entries in *Sorties* (1971), his collection of journals and new essays, reinforce the sense of concern. The journal opens, "You cannot feel your own blood run. You can feel the pulse, but not what the pulse does: not what the pulse is for," and becomes more pointed: "The sadness of middle age is absolutely unfathomable; there is no bottom to it. Everything you do is sad."

As the seventies progressed, so did Dickey's uncertainty, deepened not only by declining health, alcoholism, and the loss of physical abilities but also by the deaths of his father and mother as well as his first wife Maxine. Moreover, both *The Zodiac* (1976) and *The Strength of Fields* (1979) received generally negative reviews, perhaps owing to the fact that the enormous success of *Deliverance* contributed to the public's perception of Dickey as a novelist. In his 1979 essay "The Energized Man," Dickey continued to anguish over the effects of aging as well as the decline of his poetic reputation.

> We somehow lead ourselves to believe that the moments of youth—ah, youth, indeed!—were those times when our faculties responded and we loved and hated violently, spent sleepless nights, conceived great projects, and lived in a world of purpose which could not have existed without us. We persuade ourselves that, yes, it was nice, but it was a long time ago, and we should turn to other things: things like…well, comfort.

Dickey had lost the transcendent and was waging a war against time itself, what he had called in an early poem, "The Leap," "that eternal process most obsessively wrong with the world."

The Zodiac, a reworking of A. J. Barnouw's translation of Hendrick Marsman's "De Dierenriem," depicts a drunken Dutch poet's efforts to connect personally with the universe. Critics were quick to point out its flaws. Even Robert Penn Warren, a longtime friend, suggested that the poem lacked a defining structural principle in the opening half and exhibited some sort of structural blockage in the concluding two sections, though he argued that the bold imagery redeemed the poem. *The Strength of Fields* appeared to most critics as mostly a collection of previously published poems, a volume which Richard Calhoun and Robert Hill termed "not particularly fresh" and simply "a gathering of forces." Of the 13 poems in the opening section, ten were published prior to 1973; and the second section, titled "Head-Deep in Strange Sounds: Free-Flight Improvisations from the unEnglish," was a group not so much of translations as heightened renderings of poems by Montale, Aleixandre, Paz, and others.

As 1980 began, Dickey worked intently on *Alnilam*, convinced that after the critical and financial accomplishments of *Deliverance* (1970), he would never write a sequel and that his next novel would not achieve such success. "What I want now to do," he told an interviewer, "as far as novels are concerned is to write a resounding and interesting failure. Which is what I think this [*Alnilam*] is going to be." He was correct. Despite its 682-page length, stylistic innovation, and thematic breadth, the novel sold only reasonably well, and critical response was mixed. Having begun the novel more than thirty years earlier, Dickey had boasted that *Alnilam* would be for the air what Melville's *Moby-Dick* had been for the sea, yet the book never became a best-seller and his literary reputation remained in decline. If critics such as Peter Davison had earlier considered both Dickey and Robert Lowell as the major poets in post-World War II American literature, Dickey now found himself on the verge of being relegated to only a Southern writer. As R.S. Gwynn wrote in 1994, "If a poet does not publish any work of unquestioned merit in a quarter of a century, no amount of spin control can save his reputation from a downward spiral."

The decline in Dickey's literary reputation during the seventies and eighties resulted largely from his alcoholism, which subverted his creative abilities and encouraged work that lacked the brilliance of his early poems. Critics had praised his first collection, *Poems 1957-1967* (1967). Typical had been George Lensing's observation of the Whitmanesque affirmation in these poems, Dickey's ability to enter nature and participate in "a common vitality," a growing spirituality that enlarged his identity. During the intervening decades, however, Dickey not only lost or abandoned that afflatus but he also became focused only on projects that promised money. These were the years when he wrote large coffee-table books, commercial successes but critical failures, including *Jericho: The South Beheld* (1974), *God's Images* (1977), and *Wayfarer: A View from the Southern Mountains* (1989), as well as luxury editions that appealed to specialized audiences, such as *The Owl King* (1977), *The Enemy from Eden* (1978), and *In Pursuit of the Grey Soul* (1978). Moreover, Dickey's inability to discover new poetic directions led to poems written to order, so to speak, assignment writing for Jimmy Carter ("The Strength of Fields") and about Vince Lombardi ("For the Death of Lombardi"), the Apollo moon shot ("Apollo"), and Justice William Douglas ("The Eagle's Mile"), none of which equaled his impressive early efforts.

Gwynn's critical assessment discounted not only *The Zodiac* and *The Strength of Fields* but also *Puella* (1982) and *The Eagle's Mile* (1990), both of which Dickey had hoped would re-establish his literary ascendency. Critics, however, overwhelmingly favored his early poems despite Dickey's stated belief in and commitment to poetic experimentation. *Puella* was Dickey's first sustained effort at what he termed "Magic-Language." For "Magicians," one of two kinds of poets, he declared,

> language itself must be paramount [...]. The words are seen as illuminations mainly of one another; their light of meaning plays back

and forth between them, and, though it must by nature refer beyond, outside itself, shimmer back off the external world in a way whereby the world—or objective reality, or just Reality—serves as a kind of secondary necessity, a non-verbal backdrop to highlight the dance of words and their bemused interplay.

With *Puella*, the lyric impulse strongly reasserted itself as Dickey abandoned the anecdote to enter a new linguistic threshold that he believed had opened itself through his quasi-translations of other poets. *Puella*, therefore, becomes a seminal work in Dickey's career, endeavoring to present his second wife Deborah's girlhood "male-imagined."

The volume's involved technique is important, for the images the persona conveys depict an emotional complex inherent in certain narrative points in time that increasingly seem timeless, that is to say mythical, presenting the simultaneous penetration of worlds—male and female, present and past, transcendent and physical. Taken together, the poems trace Deborah's physical and emotional growth and reveal her heightened consciousness of the world, including her kinship with the elements of fire, air, earth, and water, and her growing knowledge of human relationships. Reviewers, however, faulted Dickey's linguistic efforts to capture and portray a mystical transcendence that frequently presented what Norman Silverstein termed merely "a questionable luminosity." In attempting a vision distinctly different from the cosmic influences in *The Zodiac*, Dickey had lost himself in his own "affection for metaphysics." Richard Calhoun and Robert Hill agreed, complaining that the poems were simply "an exercise in language" whose technique risked reader accessibility as Dickey struggled for an Otherness that was "wide-open collisionless color of the whole night / Ringed-in, pure surface."

Philosophically, *The Eagle's Mile* constituted both an extension of *Puella* in its lyrical elements and a return to the narrative anecdote apparent in the "early motion." What changed over Dickey's poetic career was not the nature of what he wanted; simply stated, he hunted not *a* but *the* central situation that would successfully evoke his general theme—the reconciliation of the transcendent with the ephemeral. His criticism of the poems of other artists, such as Anne Sexton, Yvor Winters, and Allen Ginsberg, can often be reduced to one fault—their terrible inconsequentiality because they lack the world, its inexplicable, marvelous creation and its strange, spell-casting fullness in the midst of which is the naked human response. He asserted in his essay "Metaphor as Pure Adventure,"

> I think of the poem as a kind of action in which, if the poet can produce enough, other people cannot help participating as well. I am against all mamoreal, to-be-contemplated kinds of poems and conceive of the poem as a minute part of the Heraclitean flux, and of the object of the poem as not to slow or fix or limit at all but to try as it can to preserve and implement the "fluxness," the flow, and to show this moving through the poem, coming in at the beginning and going back out, into the larger, nonverbal universe whence it came.

The Eagle's Mile continued Dickey's examination of humanity's connection with nature. The volume's title poem has as its epigraph William Blake's line, "The Emmet's Inch & Eagle's Mile," and is strategically centered to reflect the volume's thematic arrangement, a juxtaposition of two points of view, Platonic and Aristotelean, the ideal sweeping gaze of the eagle in flight and the limited stare of a man walking on the ground. Because the persona over the course of the volume arrives at an intuitive understanding of life, he achieves a "double-vision or view" and understands that both the eagle's mile and the emmet's inch discern the truth of this world. The volume acknowledges human limitations while passionately insisting that the need to strive above one's earthbound condition is undeniable, necessary, and redemptive, not only elemental but also the beginning of the artistic process. Critics, however, again faulted Dickey's experimentation with language. Herbert Mitgang, for example, in his review in *The New York Times* declared that the poetry "meanders down the page in rivulets" that only finally come together in "a rushing mainstream." Fred Chappell, acknowledging the volume's "intoxicating grandeur," nevertheless catalogued its flaws: overstated language, banality, bathos, slang, farfetched tropes, disingenuous direct address, and an insistence on gerunds.

Henry Hart, in his controversial biography of Dickey, notes that *The Eagle's Mile*, not counting the section titled "Double-tongue: Collaborations and Rewrites," offered only twenty-six poems, many short and written in the eighties (Hart ignores the fact that *Buckdancer's Choice*, which won the National Book Award, contained twenty-one poems). Hart suggested that Dickey's "dependence" on translations and his use of older poems constituted "one sign of his struggle to find new inspiration." Other critics, including Romy Heylen and David Havird, believed Dickey's re-writes were too close to the originals. Dickey, however, had used older poems in previous collections, and his interest in re-working poems written in other languages, what he variously referred to as rewrites, collaborations, or improvisations, dated back at least to *The Zodiac* and constituted part of his effort to enlarge his voice. In lectures to his poetry classes, Dickey stressed the need to "intuit" a text, attempting to achieve "the spirit of the original" rather than a literal translation. Moreover, in a 19 January 1987 letter to Ben Belitt, he discussed his methods of translation:

> [T]he whole question of translation, and the cross-pollenization of cultures by means of translation, is very large and important, and will be more so. People are not only coming forth with more translations, but with theories of translations, which is to say defenses of the kind they themselves practice. Since Pound at least, a new kind of curious form, which I try to experiment with myself, has come into existence. This is neither a translation or a completely original poem, but a kind of hybrid which for want of a better name I am tempted to call "the rewrite."

In the preface to *The Central Motion*, where many of these "translations" were collected, Dickey commented on his technical experimentation with foreign poets:

> So intense was my involvement in the imaginative release that such encounters seem to make possible that the question of "fairness" to the original texts, and their poets, came quickly to seem irrelevant, for a new order of potentiality seemed to show in glimpses: the creation of a third entity that is neither the original poem nor a literal or even approximate reading, but comes to exist by means of intuitive and improvisational powers not employed in the original, arriving out of misreading,

substitutions, leaps, absurdities, wrenchings, embarrassments, and standing at last on its own, by virtue of its own characteristics.

Robert Bly and Robert Lowell, in any event, had also reworked poems in this form.

Death, and the Day's Light does not include any re-writes, though Dickey's interesting use of "out-takes" allows him to "translate" more fully aspects of his own poems, deeper reverberations or interpretations of his own voice. More importantly, "Show Us the Sea" and "For Jules Bacon" are fitting conclusions to Dickey's career, for they focus on the same thematic concerns announced in *Into the Stone*, allude to earlier poems, and biographically center his life. Most obviously, both poems acknowledge death as inherent in Aristotelean duality and integral to nature's cycle. Yet Dickey's previous treatments of this thematic concern offered only an awareness of the many forms of death ("The Performance," "The Scarred Girl," "The Bee," "Diabetes," and "The Cancer Match"), the poet's recognition of the diminishment inherent in the passage of time and the necessary mandate to act, to *do* whatever one could while one could. As Dickey wrote in "Falling," in which a stewardess has been accidently swept from an airplane after an emergency door springs open, "*One cannot* just *fall just tumble screaming all that time one must* use / *It*." In these poems Dickey appeared at war with death, where war was not an armed conflict but a condition of consciousness, a deliberate struggle to confront time as an enemy. By contrast, however, "Show Us the Sea" and "For Jules Bacon" show Dickey's quiet acceptance of death, less a surrender than a separate peace.

Indeed, these last poems constitute nothing less than a creation, even a rebirth that occurred when Dickey stopped drinking in 1994, emerging from his alcoholism weak but sober. He had hoped that the publication of *The Whole Motion: Collected Poems, 1945-1992* would initiate a critical reassessment of his work, an evaluation of a lifetime of writing poetry. In fact, however, publication passed with barely an acknowledgement. David Biespel in *Washington Post Book World* typified the response by celebrating those poems from 1957 through 1967 and lamenting those that followed. "By the 1970s," he declared, "Dickey's work had declined and it's hard to find anyone who doesn't agree that his poetry is now uneven; the grace and control of that remarkable decade reveal themselves only here and there." The volume garnered no significant awards. Yet as Dickey now confronted his impending death, he re-established his priorities. He reconciled with his sons from whom he had become estranged and corresponded with old friends and colleagues, some of whom had become literary rivals. He also renewed his efforts to complete "Show Us the Sea" and "For Jules Bacon," poems he determined to wring from his earlier efforts and from his old self.

The origins of "Show Us the Sea" lie in summer 1977, when Dickey's son Kevin worked as a lifeguard for Beach Services, Ltd., owned by Bill Bigham, at Southside Beach on Pawleys Island, South Carolina. Dickey had bought a summer home there following the financial success of *Deliverance*, and Kevin had recently completed his freshman year at Washington and Lee College in Virginia, where he was majoring in biology. Dickey's first wife Maxine had died the previous October, and he had married Deborah Dodson, a graduate student in his poetry class, in December. Moreover, Maibelle Dickey, the poet's mother, whom he had idolized in his youth, had died in June 1977. During his visits to the Litchfield Plantation house where Kevin was staying with his fraternity brother Rob Benfield, Dickey met Tim Guthrie, a body builder and competitive weightlifter who was also a lifeguard and whose guard tower was adjacent to Kevin's on the north side of the pier in Garden City, a nearby beach. Dickey engaged Guthrie in conversation about exercise generally and weightlifting specifically. Guthrie would frequently pose and flex for his many female admirers, occasionally pointing at the lifeguard tower or some other local attraction, and, as a joke one day, posed for Dickey, who responded, "Show us the sea." During the early nineties, Kevin, who was not a bodybuilder but whose interest in and love of the ocean Dickey had written about in an early poem, "Giving a Son to the Sea," one of two poems grouped as "Messages," told Guthrie that his father was writing a poem of that title. In "Show Us the Sea," however, Dickey re-imagined the scene, using a series of integrated and gradually expanding images and replacing Guthrie with Kevin in order to offer a meditation on fathers and sons, youth and old age, and death and immortality.

"Show Us the Sea" opens with the narrator gazing through binoculars at his bodybuilding son from behind a sand dune, watching as he strikes "A hero's improbable stance." As "Kevin" poses and points to what his admirers ask him to reveal, he seems increasingly mythic, his body in its own "age / Of bronze" made of "Phidian stone" that is "burst up from sand but cast in no metal / From underground." Over the course of the poem, however, the focus shifts from Kevin to the speaker himself whose silent requests for his son to show through his poses everything on or around the beach—the sea oats, the lighthouse, the lifeguard stand, the seagull hovering above them, the conch-shell, the school of mullet, the bowling alley over the pier, the graveyard, the three dolphins, the next wave—lead to his ultimate request to "Show us the sea." If Dickey in "Giving a Son to the Sea" realized that in Kevin's love of the ocean he "must let you go, out of the gentle / Childhood into your own man suspended / In its body," he now comes to accept his own mortality and the connection he has to the world through Kevin: "I leave muscle / To you but go with you / For as long as sand will blow past / Me full of faint voices." What Kevin has given his father is the recognition, accepted finally, of "you and I and all / There is, all born and dying, forever, at once."

Central images in "Show Us the Sea" appear in Dickey's early poems, as if he were deliberately cataloguing works he wrote in the sixties, among them the lighthouse ("On the Hill Below the Lighthouse"), lifeguard tower ("The Lifeguard"), the seagull ("Dover: Believing in Kings"), fish ("The Movement of Fish"), and a graveyard ("The Escape"). Images from later poems also appear, including Maxine's death ("Tomb Stone"), a tidal pool ("Circuit"), and specific numbers ("The One," "The Three"). Moreover, the dramatic situation in "Show Us the Sea," that of an unsuspected individual silently watching another, resembles that in previous works, such as "The Signs," "Reading *Genesis* to a Blind Child," and "To His Children in Darkness." The narrative situation in "The Bee," another poem featuring Kevin, is paralleled in "Show Us the Sea." In the former Dickey saves his son from "the sheer / Murder of California traffic" by recalling the screams of his college football coach and understanding finally that "Dead coaches live in the air, son live / In the ear / Like fathers, and *urge* and *urge*. They want you better / Than you are." Dickey in the latter poem becomes both father and coach: "I stand like your life-time coach, / Stamping on the sidelines / As back of sand, learning nearly too late that over half / Of any boy's father is a coach screaming." Even "Real God, roll," the refrain that runs through "Show Us the Sea," is anticipated by its use in "Daughter," a poem celebrating the birth of his daughter Bronwen. In this long poem Dickey was attempting to summarize his career by alluding to previous characters, images, situations, and motifs, a final look backward.

Significant, too, is the poem's title, for Dickey had long been interested in Xenophon's *Anabasis* and the March of the Ten Thousand to the sea. When the Greeks, following their defeat by the Persians and the death of their leader, reached the shore of the Black Sea at the climax of the story, a scout cried "Thalassa, Thalassa"—"The sea, the sea," signifying that the worst part of their journey home was over. Not surprisingly therefore, "Thalassa" became the working title of Dickey's novel *To the White Sea*, and in 1996, as his own turbulent career was ending, he likely desired to know that he had safely guided himself and his people, both family and close friends, through the various perils. Moreover, Dickey had always loved water, whether in swimming pools or in rivers, and the sea connoted not only life's continuation and flux but also a rich and abiding mystery. Thus, to behold the sea would be a reassurance and a revelation.

"For Jules Bacon" centers on survival during warfare, a poem that evolved from Dickey's efforts as a young airman in the Pacific to improve his physique by lifting weights fashioned from discarded war materiel. Dedicated to Jules Bacon, Mr. America 1943, the poem opens with a Whitmanesque catalogue of debris lying abandoned in a Philippine junkyard, a vast dump of rusting weight:

A delirium
Of war-waste for looters
And lizards
If what you wanted was rust or the true dead
Of dead weight,

and the subsequent efforts of the speaker to build his body: "You could take these in / And make yourself out / Of them, as you have not yet been." Inspired by the cover photographs of Bacon on the September 1943 and March 1944 issues of *Strength and Health* magazine, which Dickey received during his combat service, the speaker hangs the weathered picture on a tent pole and begins to exercise, gradually enhancing his muscles until, at the conclusion of the poem, he lifts off on the nightly bombing mission, having become larger than life:

> Metal and muscle fused
> Like a new natural element
> Whose heart was joy: alive, on fire
> With each other, glowing and tight
> With identity.

This "exchange" is the same one that animated his poems in the sixties.

Though Dickey played football and ran track in high school and college, he believed his performances failed to impress his father and were inadequate when compared to those of his brother Tom, whose track abilities reached their zenith in 1948 when he qualified for the Olympic tryouts. As a child, Dickey was physically small, sensitive, and self-absorbed; he recognized and often hid his emotions, whose display he felt to be inappropriate and unmanly. By contrast, he wanted to project traditionally held masculine traits of physical strength, daring, and courage as proof of virility and manhood. In a 1959 poem, for example, titled "The Other," he bemoaned the "rack-ribbed child" that he had been, a mere "chicken-ribbed form," and recalled those efforts to re-create himself through exercise so that he might become "a king-sized shadow" who would "rise like Apollo / With armor-cast shoulders upon me." Consequently Dickey continually endeavored to build up his body through weight lifting and sports.

His interest in the male body, however, also lies within the larger context of the Second World War, which reinforced Dickey's interest in body building as a ritual of survival, for he regularly worked out in front of a mirror fastened to a tree or tent pole, lifting improvised weights. As such, "For Jules Bacon" must be viewed within the context of Dickey's war poems, particularly "The Firebombing," which depicts the speaker's guilt at his inability to feel guilt for his actions during World War II.

The protagonist of "The Firebombing" is a man "doubled strangely in time," presently riding streetcars, sitting in bars, and checking his well-stocked pantry as he envisions his enemy's world which in the past he helped to destroy. Ordinary details of his present life, in other words, recall the other locale "As I artistically sail over," fulfilling an "'anti-morale' raid upon it" by dropping "that ungodly mixture / Of napalm and high-octane fuel." Dickey's detachment at the deaths he inflicted upon the innocent Japanese population is reflected in the fact that he becomes, during those night missions, like his plane, a kind of machine. In "For Jules Bacon," however, which similarly parallels Asian and American landscapes, the speaker figuratively escapes his own death by uniting with the P-61 itself: "The runway opened / Slowly, with all its speed came forward / With the throttle, pouring into my mouth, Jules, / With no end to it, no end but life. Life!"

"For Jules Bacon" and "Show Us the Sea" reflect one another through their shared celebration of the male body against the diminishments of time, a physical war against death that includes connections to Dickey's thematic concerns of family and love. Both poems also offer a double vision, a commingling of past and present as the imagination interacts with the realities of the world as it then is. The other poems in *Death, and the Day's Light*—"Last Hours," "The Confederate Line at Ogeechee Creek," and "Entering Scott's Night"—reveal a similar integration. "Last Hours," for example, is dedicated to his brother Tom, who lies dying of cancer in the poem. Dickey is unable to relieve his brother's suffering, to ease his death, nor can any of the Civil War commanders whose lives and exploits were Tom's studied focus during his life. Rather, he urges Tom to follow Ted Bundy, the serial killer of young women whose story Tom's daughter is presently reading beside his bed: "Follow. He is helping. Go with him / Brother, he will cross you over / Better than I can, will get you there / No matter what." Though Tom has lost his war against death, imagination can illuminate a way to ease the pain and present a transition.

Similarly, in "The Confederate Line at Ogeechee Creek," Dickey presents the imaginative transformation of reality as a counter to death. On 24 December 1864, *Harper's Weekly* reported that Union forces under Gen. William Tecumseh Sherman had crossed the Ogeechee River, passing through Millen on their advance to Savannah; Confederate forces had fallen back. Dickey's wife Deborah had seen the historical marker commemorating the site and her husband had become interested in the battle. In the poem the speaker, a retreating Rebel soldier, imagines his compatriates regrouping:

> we saw obstructions
> Parallel: backwater, copper-scaled stump-chains
> Uncoiling, uniting: horror of murderous rust,
> Breastworks beating on breasts, a lost stand
> Of pine.

In their final retrenchment against forces over which they cannot prevail, the speaker remains defiant, sustained by the certainty of the illusion: "Tecumseh," he vehemently declares, "not this time."

"Entering Scott's Night," posthumously published in the 3 February 1997 issue of *The New Yorker*, sets a softer tone. In September 1996 the University of South Carolina hosted a conference celebrating the centenary of F. Scott Fitzgerald's birthday. Among the events was an exhibition at the McKissick Museum titled "Double Vision: Fitzgerald's World of Realism and Imagination," which included clothing, movie memorabilia, and other items documenting social trends in the twenties and thirties. Many of the participants wore 1920s attire; jazz from Dick Goodwin's Trio offered entertainment. Later, Museum staff used the grounds of the Horseshoe, with its towering oaks and magnolias and winding brick walkways, for croquet, cocktails, and tea. At this gathering, the speaker sees the "Interweaving / Of histories" on "this night when the past / Has not passed." He moves among the celebrants, who are "Making company as Scott would have them, / Who brought their time / Through time." Dickey senses Fitzgerald's presence "Moving in two times, among us." As in "Last Hours" and "The Confederate Line at Ogeechee Creek," he presents the possibilities of the imagination to re-create and transform, rendering the present more vital and more real than mere facts while also clearly indicating its limitations. His brother Tom will die, the South will lose the battle and the war, and Fitzgerald's "presence" is temporary. While "Show Us the Sea" and "For Jules

Bacon," as concluding poems in *Death, and the Day's Light*, depict the inescapability of death, they also reveal the redemptive quality of that light just as they acknowledge the transience of its glory.

Dickey believed in the reality of that redemptive transience, the possibility of that lie, though he always knew where it ended. Yet while he believed, life was transformed, magnificently enough.

James Dickey on Sea Island in 1942 wearing his North Fulton High School track shorts. He had just graduated from Darlington Academy and would enter Clemson A&M College that fall.

Photo courtesy of the James Dickey Estate

Above, James Dickey (far right) with the 326th College Training Regiment, ca. 1943. Below, James Dickey with his pilot, Earl Bradley, standing beside a P-61 Black Widow, ca. 1944.

Photos courtesy of the Robert W. Woodruff Library, Emory University

James Dickey in his Air Force uniform, ca. 1945.
Photo courtesy of the Robert W. Woodruff Library, Emory University

James Dickey in his Air Force uniform, ca. 1946.
Photo courtesy of the Robert W. Woodruff Library, Emory University

James Dickey waiting at the Ida Williams Library (Buckhead Branch), Atlanta, Georgia, August 1986.

Photo courtesy of Joyce Pair

James Dickey outside of his home in Columbia, South Carolina, 1987.
Photo courtesy of Gordon Van Ness

Editorial Note

To edit is to alter. Throughout his career, James Dickey characteristically corrected and revised typescripts, having them retyped when revisions were extensive. The creation of a poem was difficult, he repeatedly declared, adding that no one lived long enough to call oneself a poet, a statement which explains why at the University of South Carolina he titled his creative writing course Verse Composition. It also explains why Dickey labored so extensively on his poems and why the drafts of whatever he was working on were themselves heavily annotated. His dedication to poetry, for he always considered himself foremost a poet, was authentic and convincing. Great writing, whether his own or that of other writers, was to be cherished. "What this universe indubitably is," he told the students in his final class, "is a poet's universe. That's where the truth of the matter lies. You are in some way in line with the creative genius of the universe." Affirming the value of his craft, he declared, "We take God's universe, and we make it over our way." Had his creative and critical faculties not faltered and Dickey not died on 19 January 1997, *Death, and the Day's Light*, his final volume of poems on family, war, death, and love, would invariably have undergone further changes.

The James Dickey Papers, manuscript collection #745, reside in the Manuscript, Archives, and Rare Book Library at Emory University. Items related to "Show Us the Sea" and "For Jules Bacon" are located in Box 107, folders 3 through 21, and Box 108, folders 1 through 6, a total of more than one thousand typescript pages. In Box 113, folder 13 is titled *Death, and the Day's Light* and contains typescripts of the title page; "Conch" and "The Drift-Spell," both grouped under the heading "Two Poems: Son and His Mother"; "Last Hours"; "The Confederate Line at Ogeechee Creek"; and "Entering Scott's Night." No other new typescripts are included. Many things died with Dickey.

Dickey had published "Last Hours" in the autumn 1994 issue of *The Southern Review* and "The Confederate Line at Ogeechee Creek" in the winter 1997 issue of *Five Points*. "Entering Scott's Night" appeared posthumously in the 3 February 1997 issue of *The New Yorker*. It is possible to argue that Dickey would have altered the present arrangement of these three poems. Their order is chronological but adheres to the sequence of thematic concerns first announced in *Into the Stone*. Of his planned "out-takes," he completed only "Conch" and "The Drift-Spell," both of which he had previously published. It is reasonable to assume that he would have included other "out-takes" from among those identified in his notes. By bracketing the three poems with the two groupings, "Two Poems: Son and His Mother" and "Two Poems on the Survival of the Male Body," the former derived from the latter, Dickey offered a hermetic volume whose poems portray the cyclic nature of life. The organization of the collection, therefore, reflects its content.

"Show Us the Sea" has fifteen identifiable typescript drafts, beginning with notes and early fragments and concluding with a revision marked "Last Draft" written across the title page in Dickey's florid style along with a parenthetical notation, "Loop for 'Out-takes.'" This "Last Draft" totals 59 pages that are nevertheless further annotated with handwritten alternative wordings interspersed with typed instructions. On page 3, for example, Dickey interrupts the draft, stating, "(Note: do something with this fusing, this business of the human body and the thing it designates, becoming, for a moment, the same, Or taking on each other's qualities)." On page 52, the instruction emphatically reads: "NOTE: THIS IS RIGHT AT THE END, IN THE LAST TWENTY LINES."

"For Jules Bacon" has eight typescript drafts, though notes and early workings of the poem are missing. The eighth draft totals 70 typescript pages, all of which have handwritten annotations on them; across the top on the title page, Dickey wrote: "for both poems, to precede them: '. . .the red outline of beginning Adam' –Beddoes–." No other instructions are included in the draft.

Dickey's compositional method facilitated the writing of both "Show Us the Sea" and "For Jules Bacon." In the left-hand margins of each typescript page, he systematically numbered that "section" of the poem where the lines would eventually appear. Numbers ranged from one through ten. A working outline thus guided organization and development of the dramatic situation and enhanced organic unity of principle images. Divisions were clearly designated; one sees where a "section" ends and another begins because a 4, for example, has become a 5. However, periodically throughout the poems, lines numbered 3, for example, appear when Dickey was working on, for example, "section" 6. Some idea with respect to the earlier "section" had presented itself and he had begun to explore and extend it further by creating new variations of individual words and phrases, intending later to remove them and rework or integrate these lines into "section" 3 in the next draft.

It is impossible to determine with certainty the precise language, punctuation, and typographical format for "Show Us the Sea" and "For Jules Bacon" that Dickey would have finally chosen; the poems, in other words, are works-in-progress. The opening section of "Show Us the Sea," which *Partisan Review* had published in its summer 1990 issue and which he labeled "a fragment," is unchanged throughout the various drafts except for the accent marks which Dickey added to emphasize specific words; he wanted the poems read aloud. In editing each work, I have collated the typescripts, focusing particularly on the last three drafts of each poem and selecting the wording which repeatedly or most often manifests itself. Throughout this process, the governing principle was "Less Van Ness, more Dickey." Although line breaks, margins, and spacing are more problematic, the present arrangement reflects past Dickey practices and reveals Dickey's voice. Spelling has been standardized. In his drafts, Dickey frequently used a series of colons within a line rather than a dash or semi-colon to indicate sudden shifts of thought. I have lessened their use so as to mitigate possible confusion and enhance comprehension. Where necessary, I have also eliminated some of Dickey's use in "Show Us the Sea" of the refrain, "Real God, roll," and in "For Jules Bacon" of direct address. Finally, I have divided "Show Us the Sea" into five parts to provide a better sense of the poem's changing dramatic situation and the speaker's shifts in association. Precedent exists for such a decision. Dickey sectioned such earlier poems as "The Being," "Drinking from a Helmet," "The Common Grave," "Turning Away," "Pine," *The Zodiac*, and "The Little More" as well as a poem such as "Drifting," unpublished until Ward Briggs' edition of *The Complete Poems of James Dickey*.

That collection, published in 2013, finally allows for the possibility of a balanced assessment of Dickey's poetic career, certainly a fuller study given the omissions in *The Whole Motion: Collected Poems, 1945-1992*. That it offers previously uncollected poems and includes variants in diction and line as well as provides biographical and historical references cannot but assist scholars in recognizing the full extent of Dickey's imagination and the muscular vitality of his poetry. However, in the notes to his preface, Briggs states: "It would be possible to construct a version of 'Two Poems on the Survival of the Male Body' from the many manuscripts of that work that exist in the Department of Special Collections, Washington University Libraries, St. Louis, and in the Manuscripts, Archives, and Manuscript Library, Emory University, Atlanta, but I limit myself here only to poems published by Dickey."

No such manuscripts exist at Washington University. Following an email inquiry by Gordon Van Ness seeking clarification, Briggs responded on 13 October 2013:

> As I recall there are some ms at Washington with poems about weight lifters and body builders an early obsession of Jim's, as you know. Nothing that exactly resembles the Jules Bacon poem you've been working on, but shows the lines along which he was thinking from early days. He was floundering so on the latter years, particularly with the sad Aleixandre poems, and going back to earlier subjects of interest like Joel Cahill. Thus I think, Jules Bacon.

Dickey sold his papers to Washington University in 1964, almost fifteen years before he actually started serious work on "Show Us the Sea." To suggest that the poems about weight lifters and body builders housed at Washington University are "manuscripts" of "Show Us the Sea" is to argue that Frost's "Reluctance" is an early draft of "Stopping by Woods on a Snowy Evening" because both poems concern snow.

It might be argued that *The Complete Poems* renders publication of Dickey's final volume unnecessary or superfluous, partly because the former already includes all the short poems in the latter and partly because Dickey himself failed to complete the two long poems before he died. *Death, and the Day's Light*, the reasoning might go, offers nothing critically new or valuable. However, Dickey had made substantive progress toward completion of both "Show Us the Sea" and "For Jules Bacon," the final drafts varying not in structure but in an exact determination of sometimes tentative wording or enjambment. Then, too, he had already arrived at an understanding of what he wanted the overall organization of the volume itself to be, that is, the exact arrangement of all the poems. Additional poems, if he had written and included them, would have enlarged but not altered either that arrangement or his view of the cyclic nature of life: the reality, and finality, of death and the consequent need to live one's life boldly, courageously, and with consequence. Though that life would die, it would not die out. Thus, I would argue, his title, *Death, and the Day's Light*.

Examination of Dickey's final volume, moreover, offers additional critical approaches by which to scrutinize the poet's works. Recent criticism, for example, in gender studies would enhance an overall understanding of Dickey's focus on survival; too, much might be learned, though Dickey himself would surely have disapproved, by using Christian or theological criticism. Given the pronounced refrain in "Show Us the Sea" of "Real God, roll" and the emphatic celebration of the male body in "For Jules Bacon," it would be difficult to deny the efficacy of such approaches.

James Dickey and I were friends. We shared the belief that the origin of the creative impulse lay in humanity's religious nature, which flourished even amid the brutal and terrifying life of living like animals in the depths of caves. With great good luck, poetry could touch the sublime. In numerous conversations from 1982 until his death in 1997, we discussed literature, painting, music, cinema, astronomy, sports, politics, and family. He taught me to use a sextant. One afternoon during summer 1994, I visited his home on Lake Katherine in Columbia, South Carolina, to discuss the early unpublished or uncollected poems I had asked to include in my editing of his early notebooks, *Striking In*. We had agreed on twenty-four poems, which he had grouped and arranged in a specific order before we left his study and adjourned to the den that served as a personal library. He sat on the sofa, surrounded by a castle of books consisting of a thousand volumes in towers more than four feet high. On the other side of the room were seventeen thousand additional books, the working collection of a major poet who never stopped reading, discussing, and writing. On the coffee table lay the latest draft of "For Jules Bacon," and he kindly let me examine it, explaining his compositional methods and markings as I looked through the thick typescript. When I finished, he took the manuscript and read aloud the conclusion, emphasizing in his southern voice the final lines.

Because Dickey graciously detailed his method of revising the various drafts, the reconstruction as presented here adheres to his directions. It is the first publication of what inevitably turned out to be Dickey's final poems and thus constitutes an invaluable addition to the canon of a major American poet.

Two Poems

Son and His Mother

I. *Conch*

                Cry of something

    Forgot and empowered   intact both dead and alive:

          Gland-cry   clear, clean,
      Discreet, undiminished, hovered-in

   By you, infinitely encircling what the shudder-
       Dark under the mullet-field's spread
        Inch of undercover in the sun

      Says: inexhaustibly lost sound

      Of the shell, it speaks
        Only itself,
   Delaying, unmarveling, unmoralizing:
      Limitless last word
     Released from spiraling.
                          There is no
Whole truth, but this is what we have,

        And it goes on
Beyond impact, beyond reach, beyond recall,
         Not passing

       As I catch myself
Catching myself listening to the conch
Without the shell: the one voice, now,

For my son coming naked from the ocean,
Myself created new-human

By limit, father-rooted in sand.

II *The Drift-Spell*

When you come off the beach, son, when you leave the sea

I shall appear, without your knowing,
As you learn why and where
We are going. With no words we shall willow

Through naked tourists,
Passive nothing bodies stogged in sand
From where I watched you glory in your body
And gloried with you but are leaving
To move across the highway

And into woods: shall pass through, on
Into the open, walking in step
And out of step, into the churchyard, going where she is:
Where she lies on a silk pillow
Under moss the color of her eyes, and like them
Full of the drift-spell. Moss, son, is the grey part of silver,
Moving as though found in air

By other air, the half-alive, the half-life
Of tree-breath: precious, perilous, marking time

Over her. Your mother is here, son, with the others, amongst
The tree-hanging, wandering dead, the stomach-sway
Of swaying moss. The dead and no others are around us,
Not falling, not dying, not one of them sick, in the mild

Wilderness of the cemetery. It may be an owl
Will fly. No; there is only one, descended –
Ascended into rock. It is over your mother: it was

It is her bird, now
New on the upright of the grave
Graven, and will be here as long as stone

Will hold an image. Without words, we shall know
That we have her forever: are learning to the full
What we have: death, and the day's light,

The three of us in love. Moss,
Your mother's eyes, and an owl in stone.

Love, and the day's light?

No, she is honest with us
Anywhere, son. Death, and the day's light

With us here, full of the drift-spell.

Last Hours

for Tom

Not Stonewall

Not Longstreet

    commanders of your endless enlistment on
      both

  Sides of the Civil War

                                          but mostly South

      I have come to tell you, Tom,

That Longstreet has failed   and, as well, Melville,
   Who feared him,   has failed,   even though he said

Longstreet moves through the hauntedness:

                                   Tom, Tom,

He does not know what has come: Longstreet does not
   know

How salvation for the doomed arrives
   A hundred and thirty years later: salvation for the Civil War

Fanatic, the cancer-dying brother. Take it where you find it,
    Where it comes to you from everywhere

And anywhere, Brother. Man, I do love you past

The long-lost limits of love, but Longstreet will not do

Any longer. I know it   I have lived it: you have put your life,
Your mind, your blood, into researching the projectiles
   Of that war,

       but you are dying, now, Tom, and nothing will do

    Any longer, of the bullet-stripped trees
           Of Malvern Hill. Where should we go? The nurse

       And the rest of us?   Where?   What should we do?

    Tom, your teeth minute by minute
    Grow longer with cancer. Your tongue is white

       With suffering: Your face is an all-out skull.
            I have never seen you like this.
I see you now, Brother, floundering, sweating to struggle free

          Of the Civil War that has no more use. I have tried,

          I have held to history for a while
             Because you did, because it meant so much

To you. Watching you die, I have come to know, one more time,

    Stonewall will not help: he has no ambushing
    Military power over cancer. Munitions, projectiles
    Cannot be part of death this time, although

You could have directed their fire.

                                          The nurse has left

The white room, again, to family. Who will help? Your daughter

    Settles into a paperback.   Ah, Tom, expert
     In logistics, troop movement: your only girl settles,

Settles near and goes right by

The dead war you loved. Will your life
         Of devotion help you: life given utterly

To a lost cause? Brother, I can show you: this is my last shot.
    As I stand by your bed I am wearing
    A Confederate belt buckle you unearthed
    By map and shovel, by entrenching tool, from the red

Rain-sodden battle of Antietam

                                          and handed to me

And hand it still, and cinch it
To your brother's gut

Now and from now on out. Does it help? No.

Brother, I understand: your pain is great. No planned retreat

From it: Longstreet cannot come up, fall back, or come through

The hauntedness. Your daughter sinks into reading

And starts her voice. No more munitions,
No more projectiles, Tom. The South cannot win; but here

Here in the paperback

Is something else. In your daughter's hand for some reason
Known only to women is the step-by-step

Chronicle of Theodore Bundy. I repeat: Longstreet has failed
To help your life,

Your death. The stranger is beside you. It is Bundy moving

As Longstreet moved, but now through the hauntedness

Of Florida State. The deliberate stranger has come

In time: has come to be here

In the white room. The teeth shoot from your gums
With pain: more pain: but now you are engaged
    Beyond the artillery: beyond where you were

At Chancellorsville. This time,

Old campaigner, I tell you, I tell you and again
        Your brother does not know

    Where salvation comes from. Take it where you find it

        On your deathbed, Tom: where it comes to you

            From anywhere. Longstreet has dissolved

        Into the hauntedness. Follow now: follow
The other murderer. Listen: there is one more girl

            Walking innocently home: home
    To the sorority house. She is your daughter reading

                To you: she is the final
Unprotected girl. Watch. Wait. Follow. Follow

        The murderer, for he has caught the interest

Of your brain's last blood. Last: the last of it.
                Crouch in the last hedge

                Of Tallahassee: hover
Over the reading girl: she is part
            Of your death, glad to be so. Almost dead, now,

      Brother, you suspend yourself over her, the one girl
          Of your loins, in some form yet unknown,
Bound to the killer. Disembodied from your pain, you swim

      In air, in the last delight, as Longstreet hovered
    Through the hauntedness, your daughter the last
          Victim, as she reads to you those chronicles
              Of stalking. And while you stalk, stalk

    In midair, Brother, take this: your blood kin's last word

           Of love: follow not me
          But the murderer. He will kill
         The pain, in the one good act

Long after the execution. Follow. He is helping. Go with him

        Brother, he will cross you over

      Better than I can, will get you there
          No matter what. Follow.

              Follow on.

The Confederate Line at Ogeechee Creek

Falling back from Millen, we saw obstructions
Parallel: backwater, copper-scaled stump-chains
Uncoiling, uniting: harrow of murderous rust,
Breastworks beating on breasts, a last stand

Of pine, sawhorses, clotheslines, millstones,
Bushes tense with the hoarded standstill
Of briars. Here we took one step back, and now
None back. Slash-pines balance and lean

Into line. Every underground breath
Breaks its own hold, and will speak
Not only by granite.
                          Backwater stirs. Hawks
Hover like needles, trembling and trembling

Into certainty, all beaks and hooks
Set north. Tecumseh, not this time.

Entering Scott's Night
(F. Scott Fitzgerald, 1896 – 1940)

Interweaving
of histories:
A torso enchanted into thread. Time spun inside-
out, and worn so. A sweater only, but, as another time,
Another life shaped it.
Am I my other,
Yet, in double-time stitches? No;
Not quite; not in the looking glass. It will be so

When I step outside, this night: this night when the past
Has not passed. There
here, in the paper-lit garden,
A dark-glowing field of folk, the dead, the celebrants
Making company as Scott would have them,
Who brought their time

Through time. Wearing the inner skin
Of a sweater, ghost garment, I am with them,
Some flying from the thing they feared, and some
Seeking the object of another's fear.
On fountain-shifted ground, among straight bricks
Woven serpentine into walls,
In leaves and lamp-light and time,
In the grass-lamp glow

Of hedges, all are still,

And a hooded spark from lanterns
Travels from glass to glass, from eye to eye
Like intuition. It is Scott's,
Moving in two times, among us
As we stand fountain-raining, imperilled
In celebrant stillness, with the shadow of a woman

On serpent-stone totally dancing.

Two Poems on the Survival of the Male Body

...the red outline of beginning Adam
Beddoes

I *Show Us the Sea*

I

                Real God, roll
                                            roll as a result
Of a whole thing: ocean:

                        This: wide altar-shudder of miles

                Given twelve new dead-level powers
          Of glass, in borrowed binoculars, set into

                The hand-held eyes of this man

          And no other, his second son coming to his head

              Like Armageddon, with the last wave.   Real God,
Through both hands and my head, in depth-bright distance, roll
                    In raw caught sharpness

              Of sight, and let my son come,
Exploding with proximity, and with him bring voices
     Faintly around him, the sounds not matching
The size of their magnified bodies.   No harm; I am invisible

              With sand.   The sea, only, is on-coming
                  Face-on, with my boy's
              Impact incandescent on my head
                                    as he strikes

A hero's improbable stance: flesh that would be bronze,
     Be stone, the form of stone, struck from within

     The stone.   Statue, yes: a creature lured into being
          By gestures it has chosen in its sleep: my son with all
Statues, toiling with existence where they stand
               At dead of light.

                    Seventy yards off,
But at my brow, he poses, and with each pose, points

To what the others around him, in wind-frail voices, ask
     To be revealed.   It is a game.   He sets his pose

               To that, his whole body distinct
     But fusing with it.   Show us the lighthouse, they cry.

                    You brace, you earnestly freeze.

          Show us the lifeguard's chair, they call
On the small-tongued and varying wind.   Your muscles near
          The soul of your body, and grip,

                         And the sound of voices
Changes the wind: some small, unnamable human-spirited sound

     In frail stage-murmuring voices calls you to point, to name
          With your body something the world still has to show
     And establish by the still-down of your muscles.

                         Show us the sea,
          They ask.   Show us the lifeguard's chair
                    With the draped sandy towel.   Show us

The bowling alley on stilts over the school
        Of mullet.   Show us the crab and the gull, they cry.

                Muscle-up and stop
The sun on a dime, where it is: noon: the highest place

        It can get.   Show us the gull
Against the cloud before the wind moves it.

             Come forth in stamped, stunning veins
As though there were a hover of hammer-sparks
        Around you like silica in the born-again eagle eyes
Of your hidden father.

        Your stance brings from you
Phidian stone, and covers it with sweat, in lens-light
        A focus like tightening the gut that shows

My son unfairly close, in his age
        Of bronze, burst up from sand but cast in no metal
From underground.

        Show us the gull.   The lighthouse.
You and the tower fuse.   You and the bird.

           Show us the ground
    Where we stand.   Show us the dune blowing off
And staying, cloudy with grains.

In your young wild sweat, from the feet
        Up, each sand-grain goring like flint, your body flinches
    Into full definition: alive, stationed like Antaeus

　　　　For renewal, sweat-shine on you
　　　　　　　Like merited power　　choked　congested　　strangling
　　　　Into muscle, youth-metal:　　　the straining motionless figure
　　　　　　　　　Bunched and pointing at something

　　　　　　But also at something yet to be sent
　　　Into the world.

　　　　　　　You crouch and overcrowd yourself
　　　Toward the tower, the engine-parts look
　　　　　Of a body-builder's body.　　Your shoulders concentrate,
　　　Knit like a brow. You bunch with paralyzed maledom.

　　　　　Show us the conch-shell.　　Show us the stripes
　　　Of the lighthouse.　　Show us the sea-holly.　　　Show us
　　　Vacation cottages in sea-oats.

　　　　　　　　　　　Show us the next wave turning up
　　　From the clear thorned field of the far-out,
　　　　　More secret, more explicit than life:

　　　　　　　Its fire-hanging arrival　　　　tunneling overstall
　　　　　　　　　throw-down of shade
　　　　　　　　　　　　　　on-pour　　　underthrust
　　　　　　eroding　　　in-rushing

　　　　　　　　　　　　　　the working, overstressed sun
　　　Like muscle-tone, indivisible.

　　　　　　　　　　Your admirers wheedle, and you fix
　　　　　　Anywhere:　on the lighthouse　the gull in its hover

For uptossed bread, drawing your shoulders together,
              As up from the last wave.

    Show us the beach-ball and the shell.   Show us
The umbrella's desert shadow.   Show us the barbell.   Show us
      the one bird rising
          Over us on sea-wind.

             Show us the tire-slick
Overturn of the dolphin.   Show us the starkness of the claw
     With no crab.   Show   show
While yóu can.   Show.   Don't change, but fix,

  Son, and through it all
            Roll, God.   Roll.

   Death comes to life
Once more, stopped dead in its tracks like the sun
   At noon for three minutes, more body-life than the body
Was meant to have.

             Alive, superhumanly
Like death, you fuse into light, quivering with more
   Than allowable life, more beautiful than the Belvedere
Burst from beach-sand, crowned with sea-holly.

    Show us the whelk and the conch   anything staying
In the world with us   pitched   quivering   wild with muscle.

        Show us the urchin
From the sea   bladderwrack   dulse   kelp   sea-weed sea-grass
      sea-holly   sea-oats.   You set

              Your shoulders to it, concentrate with possessed
                        New muscle, pointing to what can still be found
To be part of the world: the gull, undetermined, hung between
              the hollow

              Sweeping sides of height: air-
                        Paralyzed with turning, where my son points

              To it, equally still, as if he also were air-
                Paralyzed with spirit and balance: points to the gull

     As something not ever going from him, wind-borne,
But the bird is gone.   You fix on cloud alone

              As you move and draw
     One pose from the stillness of another, your body crowding
For light   for more definition   for the muscle-groups sweating
                     To define you.   Come forth

              From moving so much pig-iron
          In place: lived   lowered   lived   lifted
     Lowered   re-lifted: your body in its varied sets and sweats

                        Of muscle, as you turn and strike the sun
              Full in the face with your back, like Phoebus Apollo,
                   On the best day he ever was the sun.

                             Show us the pair
          Of sandals.   The towel over the jeep-seat.
                 The lifeguard's chair, his love-seat by starlight.

                             Show us the dead-man
          Of the crab.   The ghost-shell

                  Of the loggerhead.   Show us the human
       Fisherman.   Show us the ultimate hook.

  Show us the lighthouse.   Show us the gull, your latissimi flaring
  With the whole bird: bunching, earth-bound as for liftoff,
                    Hover of all worked muscle, working through.

  Show us the sea: its overwrought, seething approach.   Show us
            the moon by sunlight
                    in the clean clutch and bite-down of muscle

  All over you: mail-fisted stance   gauntleted   posing, pausing
            In body after body of your life.

            How you have turned yourself bright
  With sweat, made yourself whole.   Your round muscles

         Pierce through, drop-forged forth, come
                Together, as from shattering, assembling
  Sheer out of chaos by something other than human will.

                        My gaze like silica around you,
            Watching over your shoulders like hammer-work, yet soft
                    And loving as I can make it, the sea behind you

  At the same time blanking and breaking. Your mother between us
            Gone forever, and around you

  The black horizon tensing like a mainspring,
        My dying body and your dead mother's mixing
     In you, in the sun.

                Show us the gull, before its head is torn
    Clean away on the downwind, everything following
           Before it straightens and heals
With new slant.

                Show us the rough-cut of minnows
Struggling, dazzling the surface just over them,
      Alive in their perilous nerve-stand where it is,
And is gone from, in underwater mid-space.

        Show us the heron, black-footed with ripples.

            Show us their herd-swerve, instantaneous
Parrying order sheer in the needles
      Of nerve-light, slewing for open sea, blind with sun,
    Their swinging tranced as a compass,

   Who might have had, that instant, a rammed glimpse
Of a whole thing: fragment-glitter on their whole-sided herd, the full
        Half-force of undersunk light.

              Show us
The backrush dragging like shovels.

     They call for the world, that you should strike the far side
Of your deepest pose: a body, at last,
      For the whole of light.

             I call you what stands in human form
Though you shall be in your time what I am now, dying

Of time: that this should arise
                From among themselves as from sand, released
    Blazing, to show them the world

  At the sun's highest point, where the world stands most
                        Point-blank in its things than any time
    Known to Time.

            In your work with iron, the gull overhead is caught
Beyond naming, and released
        Full to the downwind, stalled-out in your latest thews.

        Show us the overwrought wave, to your father as good
  As the last.   Show us the solar silt of the runback.

                And everywhere, the endless underfoot
Hunt of the other creature under the blazing
            Overlay, cornerless and everywhere to the death.

                        Behind you, son, the eye-
    Lash glint of minnows as they swerve, coming off
            A thousand-sided flash.   On the floor, sand-ridges
        Like laid-in wind.

        Show us the splintered legs of the pier.   The tide-pool
Nerving with ripples: clear nervous universal light bright-patched
        Unparticled water, striped, stamped like a zone.

            The ripples roaming, underfoot,
                            with an element of soaring.

    More than half your body created by dead weight and work
                And will, half by your mother's and mine,

Long ago.

    Sea-orchard glitter.   Self-lifting waves.   Repeating.

II

This is the second birth
        Of the second son, brought on
    By will, by a sand-hidden man and the dead, and weight

Entirely dead, all working together: the thick ringing
        Of barbells, ringing with nothing but heft.

Your mane heifer-haired, your chest shaved blindingly close closer
        To the sun, Heaven's brown side
    Of gold, of what might as well be Heavenly power.

                Your blinding stake-out, the plough-boy
Stance, your sectioned stomach heaving
    Like something ploughed out and embodied as you flow
  From one gold pose to another.

              Show us the gull, the uptoss of bread
Cast not on the waters but the air.   Show us the gull that plucks it
    From the top of its hang-time.

                Show us the running ale
Of the shallows.   The shell-shape of the sail.   The multiplied
  Demon-driven inch of the shore-slanting ripples.

    The swales undercut between crests, all water come back
On itself by combining with the moon.

The trench-running flame of the shallows.   The hookless,
    incurable gleam, incredible
  Long-handled flash, sunlight's headlonging stand-off.

    The conch's long unsearching stare of sound,
        As though the inner ear were unwinding,
Straightening at last, as promised, the wave turning according to
    its law.

                                Its swaling looseness
            As the conch-sound swérves to be previous
                        To all other sound, the ultimate
            Inside sound, outstays the air, outstays the inner ear,

            Speaking back as it should, giving the sound
    Of a whole thing: deep   direct
Unquestionable.

                The million-thorned light on the waves!

        God flashing like chain: God, if He could flash
    Like this, like light on a link-belted, laid-open fence.
    Unparalleled meaningless power.

                        That my son should be glorying
In posture after posture in the sun.   The wheat-sheaf brightness
        and stir.
                            Over you

        A gull passing broadly, taking bread from the air
    As from the hand, all hands rising with that bread, placing itself
            Where it belongs: claiming, as it must, the essential

    Thread of the downwind.

       Voices like runners': a sense in the wind
Of words calling in mid-stride, as of air being run-through by souls
        All but human.

           Show us the tracks that we came from
In flight, in search.   By means of sand and wind, I hear them.

       Show us the knot of the dune grass,
   They call.   I see you turn, unship and clamp your shoulders.

        You point to the bird as to something not ever
Going from you.   It opens   goes forever
      On the downwind.

        Your chest set level in manic power and health
That once held the frail-haired blond soft child.

               The sun striking off
The shoulders of all-male bronze, the horizon tightening
        One turn of the screw more, around you.

     Your body-counting, heart-counting rhythms. The savage
Crouching and towering. Your seamless shifts from power-
    Pose to pose, from body to body

        Of yourself.   Incessant weight repeating
Rising and falling   subsiding   falling   subsiding
    Re-rising.

   Your muscles as though beamed to you and assembling
Only by non-light, from deeper within

    Sunlight than the sun, raw-set in you.

                      The raw green of waves rides up,
Topples   whites-out   out of the unemptied break-up of vastness.
  The swilling ripples cresting with air-white, off-side
               Of new wind.

                          Show us the dead-man
Of the crab.   The ghost-shell
    Of the loggerhead.   Show us the ultimate hook as you arch
   And point.   Bring out the hard-earned parts

  Of yourself, the improved parts of what I gave
       Of a whole thing, in a clear night twenty years back,
As the wave unsheathes, skins back
             The solar silt of the run-off in eaves of water.

     The serious strength of your feet
        Gripped on hard clean sand: one flat-footed, one

          Down-toeing for emphasis, sand moving
   With wind as something earthless
    Beside the savage and spring-bubbling runback.

The laid-out horizon, the one pressed
Merciless line: in a power-ring searching with muscular power, with all
     Of the circle as if pulled, just in time, out of chaos.

     The heart-muscle blanking through,
  Your muscles catch as though overtaking you
             from behind, a kind of primal focusing,

         And the sun unwoundingly strikes   strikes

Your set-screw stance, and now you clamp.   Your muscles tighten,
      Brighten with overstrain, dead certain from every place

        There is by means of your mother
          And me.   Cloud passes: the sun now suddenly
  Closer   cleaned   struck bare again   catches on you

      From everywhere, as though called down on your head
And body, seamlessly thewed.   Real God, roll.

                                    I see
    What I never have had, but must have had
        It in me to give, somewhere in the past, in the night.

        The sun fully fuelled for noon.
Sea-water salt and sweat-salt
  Shining like one another. From the feet, each sand-grain
    goring like flint.

                            The gull
    Laid-out by the downwind.   The conch's cry, unhealable
Even by Time.

III

            For I, too, was once
Not stogged in sand and fat but, like you,
      Hard on the hard.   I was where the minnows ran
For the sea from the flame-trench of the shallows.

                I showed what was there without
Your power-poses. Without so much body but with whatever
    Intensity I had from youth, I watched from hard sand

The small fish, their razoring side-swipe,
                 Herd-running wide open for open sea,

    And I have been both in and under
    The bowling alley racked on its stilts, thundering
                Over the mullet.

                            You grinning,
  Saintly with overstrain, unfractured, blind as a statue
            Emerging from the heart of stone
On will like hammerwork: lock-jawed and good-natured line.

        Your quartered stomach pulsing like an inlay.
Your lethal self-possessed crouch. Your harbored crotch. Your hair
    Like pounded fence-wire and sorrel.   But it is too late,

   For sweat is all over you, shining intently
       With renewal, the sun striking off what you have made

            Of yourself, with yourself, from weight
   Entirely dead, from all possible
      Repetition, from free-standing free will.

The waves' embodying gather and power.

                        Show us the lighthouse.
  The shark hounding clean.   The dolphin rolling, rounding
         Over itself.

 Still-life power.   Flax-powered head.   Fusion.   Bleak
    Exuberant pain.   The countless, counted repetitions:
Chin-ups   sit-ups   inverted curls   slant-board grimaces.

　　　　　The jaw-clench and stomach-clench bound together.

　　　Barbells:　the hold-back in their mass, the power to change
　　　　　　　　The body you were born with.

　　　　　　　Your belly in four-part armor on the flat sand,
Leached-out, exhausted with blinding. The horizon
　　　　In full open-tensioned light, striking the full set
Of muscles just in time:　one-sided rolling-dead light.

　　　　　　　　　　　　　And now the whole body's
　　　Come here, wild with work
　　　　　　　On this blazing sun-knotted image,
In thís light　on thát chest　on the goatish and brilliant hair.

　　　　　Now sand, and still　　still
Universal new-stalled light and I in it hidden somewhere.

　　　　　Show us the sea.　　Show us the down-thrown sun
Flexing like a glide-path.　　Show us the silent and final
　　Aircraft, ten thousand feet of spiritless air over us.

　　　　　　　　　　　　Show us the trackless rust
　　Of the beach, the road of it.　The instantaneous solar daring

　　　　　　　　Of your pose, the motionless vibrating search
　　　　　　　　For the true body.

　　Flock-flickering.　　Frail body-light
　　　Inlaid and primed, never overshooting.　　Show us all one side
Of gold as the minnows shoot, swerve and resolve, laid bare

　　　　　　　　　　In blitz-glitter, ready to fall

From itself, and come back, refocusing again somewhere else,
    A gold-sided cloth of pure terror
      That stands trembling in the world's greatest water.

                                  Stand whole
And imperiled.

        I have walked above them. I see them now
Not as you do, not posing to show them, but from sand
      Concealment: the beach, haunted now with muscles.

      I am watching you while your ages
               Of bronze come over you one after one,
Your pectorals rounding, your biceps contracting, all straining to be other
            Than what was born   born

      Of the orgasm's lost swivel-thrill   lost
In darkness, where it most thrives.   The connected truth, striving
  to be other than what was born.   Other   other
    Unmerciful.   Real God, roll.   Roll.

I stand here watching, son: watching
              For the dead and living that are yours
     And will be yours because of a whole thing.   Stand watching

         With the gull   with the towel   with the sun.
And I am here, like you,
       Lock-jawed with concentration   with witnessing,

         The sea-wind finding in my mouth
A strange other tongue, a new language to go with the cries   to go
    With the sound of the conch-shell.   Show us the shell.

Show us the dance pavilion.   The bowling alley
            Raised from the inlet on bow-legged stilts.

    I stand here,
            in iodine- and catspaw-glitter, rallying   striving
To be empowered in the eye-stand of stolen and honest bright distance
        Without enough time in the world.

                        What is lost, enlarges
    Toward us, the wave's over-handed dazzle, the sun-track
            Sprung, headlonging like a runway. I watch   watch
                You and beyond.

                    Dolphin: your pose takes and fixes
Him in his overroll: gold on black, like a headlight on a wet tire,
    Unembarrassed, basking in overroll, in foraging shine: one

    Then two of them
        Paralleling in overroll, coming out
                One, two, three of them evenly, exactly
        Right.

    You, son, are still. They are in their motion: there
            Where you point, your bent arm quivering
        With health.

                    Bright, twisted sorrel-like hair,
    Not mine, but your mother's: your mother's

And that of your mother under live oaks and moving moss, gray
            Slow-swarming space, drifting forever
Without body, above her, above the grave.

                      On the stone the carved owl blazes,
Seeing nothing, but claimed and riding
      Her stone to the end of the earth when it comes.

                              And my own body
That blazed once with the unknown
            Of a child going for the all-out, and struck you
Off like a clean hit straight out of light on a coin-face.

                                    The horizon
    Fades from my shoulders with cloud.

                            Show us the sand-castle's
     Shoreless foundations   slack parapets
        Hog-wallow battlement   its slackening
      Hold on the beach   its dream of stone.

My red stunned vacation shirt blown hollow and healing
                    With wind-calm, like a sail.

     The wave's falling bright-out   hanging   unstraining
Dying overcrop and you
              Fine-tuned and passionless.

                    I stand, not stared-down, annealing
   The same as you, son, with heat-light
           And below us both, the sea,

  The totally-felt free country too deep for the sun, endlessly
     Alive with the death-hunt.

   Teeming, unforced: the tide-pool's shattered stare-down
Bright with excessiveness.

                              And I, behind sand, bivouacked
In the emboldening wind.   The run-back's cowed tumbling minerals.
             The shells stumble backward down their infinite
                                         slight downhill.

The sand's unmuscled soft power   shapeless   shadowless
             And I wishing for my male glands to fill up with time
   Past, and shudder with it instead of being
                  Slowly dead with dying maledom.

              But not yet! when in these glasses my son is coming
  In like the tide
             and the father hidden like prey

   And like stalker and coach, having caught my second son
          In God's blast-furnace openness.

                                       Show us the sea,
The voices mingle and say. Show us. Show us. I bend and narrow
          The glasses on you, listening
   Universally with the formlessness of sand.

          I stand like your life-time coach,
                                        stamping on the sidelines

    As back of sand, learning nearly too late that over half
Of any boy's father is a coach screaming   wringing his hands

Protesting   throwing his hat down   praising   weeping
             Cursing for loss   loss   witnessing what you did
          Without me, beyond me: for not knowing

What to do, what to advise, but most of all for not knowing
    What to say that will help,

Buried to the lips in sand, counting
    His years, and not enough: the gull and your father, equally
      Balanced, equally still, hands focusing

    On you, with razor-and-nearly-prophetic sight blown into
The hill where his feet are buried,
    His head in the wind with voices and sand.

        Why is it I hear, in this wind also,
Time like the cry of the conch,
    Unbreakable, broadening to the inmost?

    The boy's body points.   Show us the sea.

    There is nothing   nothing
But the massed by-pass of wind not missing me.   It is lost

        And lost, streams off me backward
With one bird giving openly its wings to the downwind,
    Leaving bread in the air   turning broadly

        Incurving over, remaking
The downwind in a strong curve.

        Show us the sail
Rounding, repossessing the wind
    From the other side: the boom swinging   the sail coming true
Once more as the boat comes about   turns   reborn.

        Show us the dance

            Pavilion over the inlet.   How far did we dare to dance
                        Over this grey water?

            Show us the bowling alley,
                        Where the great ball blanks
         The small timber down in helpless windrows.

                              The pins, in their blanketed fall
         Of pyramidal wood   the great ball striding with swerve
                  The hoarded shock like a closed booming wharf

   Over the free loom of mullet under the planks
                        Now shorn, now nowhere: not dazed
        By the thunderous black-out of the world's total timer.   My son,

                  I have been everywhere you point:
         Where the long high hooded alley resonates like a wharf,
                  Trembling with shock, like straw.

            The hacked cloven ball   the inboard rumbling
         Pent and booming   the great ball's tongue-and-groove swerve
                  The doomed wood thriving on impact

     The elevated ball returning,
                        Groove-running backward to the source.

       With this much love from the hidden, light falls
                  From wave to wave and rises, right-bodied.

             The gull in its covering hover.   Your mother's death
       Accepted, moss-moving.   My eyes moving where our son seizes

His uttermost self, and points to part of a whole thing seen
        In secret, from sand.   Show us the grave and the moss.

IV

Coming back to the son: created by the living and the dead
   But the best of him by his own hand.   Those glory-crouching
Overcrowded muscles in the sun: they can change

        But not advance.   You are still, son,
  In your pose, the wind staying faintly all over me

                      With voices and passing
   Where I arched and blazed once in the middle
        Of age, as a gull gives up its body
Once only to the real wings, and the downwind is there.

  I try, as I can,
    The same body-slant, bedazzled with dying and immediate
Vision, clearer than hindsight, twelve powers closer to being
     As keen as God's, and all the time on my son, remembering

   When the male glands, at their best,
      Or near it, foreshorten and let go, let come
   What will.

You have something of mine I left for you to change as you would
               By sweat and will: left it in the dark
  Of a bright-out with a woman, somewhere in the on-go
  Of a whole thing.   Real God, roll.

 To feel the whole and true air run   feel the entire
        Sand-shifting turn of the earth.

    Sand, with its other side always
                Moving in on it, always coming
  Behind you, shifting with earth-turn, and on your shoulders
                The horizon seamlessly swarming.

              To be given total and terrible eyes: I leave you
      With your arms jammed with high hammers,
    Watching from here, as I do, from seventy years,
Seventy yards. Hunch-backed with solitude, I may have been struck

              For the last time with awe
                    At being in there   in here with you
              And all of it.

                And you, your pumping, your throttled strangling
With weights, your cork-screw wrestling
          With the Nautilus, emerge with yourself, from yourself.

              In one twelve-powered sweep, I keep coming back
To what is behind you: wide surround of miles
        Beyond time but always in place
                        out to the shuddering clear limit

            And then back to my son
    In his age of bronze.

      Myself dying of no known sickness
Or wound, but of age, of the world's going through you and leaving

          You, at its own pace, in its own
    Rhythm: the death of part of a whole
        Unkillable thing.   Real God, roll.

                              But you, my son,
Caught by yourself in mid-bronze, locked into that part of the world
            You point to: Show us the sea.

                                    Show us the ghost-shell
            Of the loggerhead.

                                    And I, behind sand,
Blowing with every grain of its blow-away power in my body, and all
                  Its blow-by as well.

        For you cannot make out your father blowing like sand
            And age and death.   No. He is not there. Or here.

        Against your clear body, I have survived to this point
                            And no other: survived
            The heart attacks   the strokes still waiting, their chances
                Getting better with fat.   The cancer

                In the air, in the sun, in the food
            Of my time, in most things I breathe, but not
            This wind, son;   I don't believe it.

                                            The others
            All waiting also, their chances getting better
                With pollution and the deep-frying fat of pleasure.

        And deep in your own toil
                      And toils, in your passionless bondage
        To yourself, bound-down in muscles, your mother dead
                and your father dying of sand, but whole
            At this one moment: Death, and the day's light.

       I cannot move, or move
From you, tunnel-visioned, until you break the point,

The link with the world: your father
      Here, in the furious sun, my whole male blood dying
  But raising you into focus.

              Your positioned pointing,
The struggle with your body, made of noon-light, to name the world

           As you wait with me, gaining in potential
For death, with each heartbeat, as one by one they fail
                              To find me.

    Paralysis hovers in my fat
            Not like a gull, but I am your father
      Still, and with you I watch, turning

           To the lighthouse   the mullet   the bowling alley
To the shell of the loggerhead's ghost: in all of it, turning

       Toward the things of this world like a flower
             To the sun and with you for this moment
       In all of it.

                 You have made of the whole body
Of light a cry for help   terror   love   lostness.
  I can tell you nothing. I cannot hold

    Your muscle-drunk form in my arms
        Or the powerful light of your youth. I cannot come clear
      Of sand and fat: come clear

From behind the sand blowing graveward
Toward the hanging moss.

    The impotent gland-deep cry. The meaningless
     Unstoppable cry of the conch like the unknowable
Itself, wide-open and dreaming: the beginning
     Word of the whole truth. Real God, roll.

      The gull trued up and taken
   Alive by the downwind, going with it
     Into the all-out.

Soft-soled with sand, I cannot reach you. The others can come
  To you, but not your father.

  The slur of the shallows. The inlet's grind-down
   Of the tide-pool. The sea forever beyond
 Blanking and harvesting. The grey spindrift
     Light as moss, full of the drift-spell.

    The moss: silver overborne
Loose drifting: the half-breath of trees, of bedding released from
    all sleep
And risen, but only so far as any branch.

In the mild wilderness of the cemetery, your mother motionless
  But drifting with moss.

  Lord, I wish there were some way for her to see
     Your body here, its drop-forged sheen,
Its wheat-sheaf brightness and stir, your postures,
    The stillness of utter life.

                              The graveyard plotted
            With shadows, your body shadowless as wheat.
                  Set yourself in your one pose
                     Beyond all others.   Show us the sea

                                    Before you clamp down
            With all you have.   Show us the graveyard.   Show us

      The whole thing before another man appears, set free by you
                     To live, to stand not young but in an age
      Of bronze, who takes your assembling shadowless pose,
Pointing where you would point.

                                 One can think of the world
            As it most truly is: something to be shown to us
                  Only by all humanly possible moves

      And all that buried wild-life hunting
                        And hunted hard in all that silence beyond,
            Out of the wind.

                           I can think only of the soft child
                  In its blond sleep, the graveyard, all shadow-
      Drift and flotation, and you shadowless,

                              The stinging, soft
            Utter blow-by of sand, and your father hidden in wind
Full of the passing voices of young strangers.

                                             I have seen
            The sail as the prow ripens keenly.

                                                I have seen

Before what you point at: the world in this exact high light
                    Where you strike it in pose after pose,
    As though this were the first day.   Through you

        I will always be coming back, like the next wave
Coming straight at you out of the world.

    You have remade your body in every position
                From what I had to give.
        These will fall from you
                    In the time that has hidden your father in sand,

                            When the thin cries come
        Over me, blowing past, the gull giving itself
            Whole-souled and slant to the downwind.

            Son, uncowed, cow-licked, blond muscles primed
    With black shadows, latissimmi broadening and braiding,
        Flaring, foreshortening, spread like a bird's body, giving
            Whole-souled to the downwind.

                            The runback
    Moving, outsweeping the shells.

                        V

    Cloud passes over and then off. My boy's body catches the sun
                Anew, where it lives, at the exact
                Instant the tide-pool unlocks its light,
                    The sun headlonging on its track.

                            Show them how the wind comes
            To life by means of their voices   how the sun tracks

    And untracks on the waves, God-burning, unknotting
                      In various slacks, the struck sail heeling
  Its blind other side with new wind,
        Rounding and filling out, like muscle.

        The far sail pauses, wandering
    Like moss, the strong air fulfilling itself in cloth.

    The gull's hammerheaded heeling, slide-filling
Full into its utmost wings, combining stall-out and rounding.

      Stillborn in death, but swaying
            With moss, your mother drifting, travelling
Alongside the others until the stone itself moves like moss.

                        I have seen anew the cloud
    You showed   the tower   the lighthouse
The lifeguard's chair   the bowling alley   the wave.

I have seen the cloud and the cloud
        Of moss.   Show me the cloud
    That never moves, and is gone

Where the dead move always among themselves:
Never fail   never fall   never drop their poses, even for every power
            Up to twelve, eyes full of dying and human love.

                Show me the dead moving the moss
Without wind. It takes no muscle, son, to rejoice. As it happens,
      I am rejoicing without muscle, without any youth

      But yours.   I leave muscle

To you but go with you
            For as long as sand will blow past
        Me full of faint voices.

Beholding it, I feel my heart
            Shoot into the breast of the bird
        Over you in the downwind. I feel you go through me,
            And I come back nearly, very nearly, forever.

                    Show me once more
The bright side of sweat and your mother's not acceptable death
            Accepted, moss moving.

        Her eyes—I know it—still
Full of the drift-spell as in death's totally clear
            Other-empowered eyes.

    And if it happens that I am rejoicing
        In every position, I will still be hiding,
    Son, for a while and beholding

    Every pose with clear-headed eyes, blowing backward
Off himself like a dune.   Show me the sand I am in.   Show me
    the dune
            Where your father peers, still

    As death, but alive, proud of your orchestrated muscles; yes,
And of the world as it so clearly is, and of myself in it with you

The rest of the way: who made you

    Beyond and by impulse with no idea of you, of the changes,
      Or of the changes of the highest light
And your staged, staged-waiting body.

    The wave delivered out of entirety, out of the blue
Of all the world's wild original fury-making of form, not for all
      twelve powers of human love:

                          Oncoming
      Effortless
                                      Out of the world

                      When the last wave overthrongs
        And falls
                falls   lulls
Lugs   grovels   thins and backslides here, or anywhere.

              Simple pool-splinters of fish trapped in water
By hard sand.   The stoked transparent out-drag.

                                  The dolphin
      In the rolling beast-slick of its body.

    Even your last pose, the one pointing

To the noon sun itself, still needing some origin, still needing
    something from me, as the last wave falls.

    In the brute vital laying-on of light
      No fragment missing, as though made of Time itself,
As I am almost out of time, as well, at twelve o'clock, in twelve lights.

    Show me the sea exactly in time

And give my excessive eyes and powers back where I got them

   Before I put them down for good, as I would give
      Away my life, and you and I and all
  There is, all born and dying, forever, at once,

        Of a whole thing.   Show me the sea,
Second son, for the one time: the one time
         Of all.   Real God, roll.

            Roll.

II *For Jules Bacon*

      All junk there is
Consists of whole parts, and this holds: holds true and creates
In wars, great dumps and yards,
Fields and sumps, swamps

Of it: holds: holds and keeps,
I tell you, ravines   gulches
Suck-holes   lowered gardens
Lower than the low part of Hell,
Hills and valleys   pastures
Cut-banks   washes   arroyos   gulleys
Rammed, jammed with mortal metals, Jules,
From whole C-47s down

To point-o-seventeen wire.   Everything gets thrown in
And on, at will, or the other side

Of will, none without stain: cylinders
With cooking-steels, hubs, tubs, nubs, post-hole diggers,
Basins, tools,
Tool-tools, no-tool tools,
Wheel-bases, swill-pails,
Spokes, spikes, chains,
Chain-link fence-parts, wash-buckets
For breeding lizards, pails, garbage-cans, oil-cans,
Swivels, pulleys,
Rivets, bushings, rods,
A delirium
Of war-waste for looters
And lizards
If what you wanted was rust or the true dead
Of dead weight hid-down:

Fuel-pumps, copper housings, jointed
Hoses, Jules, steam-fittings, mountings and cowlings
Of all kinds: an Eden
For squatters' rights: unlooted
Landing-trucks, propeller blades, sidings: if you could use
Tires, braces, stays, jeep-parts, pistons, cables,
Lard-cans, GI cans, a beer-
Bottle, dashboards, floorboards, wing-struts,
Bath-tubs, wash-tubs that have held
The one true-balancing
Wholesale weight of the true blue South
Pacific.   Scrap-iron, pig-iron, clutch-plates, armor-plate
I was looking

To loot, Jules, to rob the dead
Metals, and come up
With a self.   All these had mass.   All these could become
Part of a new human body
Made from the old.   You could take these in
And make yourself out
Of them, as you have not
Yet been.   A looter's paradise
Except that there was no use
For any of it, unless you think
Your body might be alive
And waiting in crankshafts and gears
If you could live
Long enough to lift it out.

                    Standing there, I said
To myself, who was still living, this junk can be better
Than if the metal were eaten

And turned into you,
                     and stood up
And lived and shed light
Like oil, like life,
Of what, all the time,
You had it in you
To be, but could not find
Outside the junk-yard.

Rust: lock-rust, weapons-rust, gun-rust, brass-rust: my loot
Of rusting weight, a blitz
And swill of dead metals: my body-to-be
In the lock-rusting scraps, the dull dazzle
Of galvanization, before plastic
Took over the gulleys of the world.

I was searching for the most potent
Weight, the weight most suited
To "my stage of training,"
Jules, which was at the start
Of everything: weight that would do it
For me, Jules, with what little I could bring
To weight   to rust   to any engine-part I found
Left to its weight
Alone: bring out the untapped best
In me, if there was one. I had to gamble
That somewhere in me there must be
A body better than this one
                     better than the one
I stood up in
Over a sunken continent of junk,
Better than the skinny kid beginning to turn
Sand-colored with atabrine. For my money,

My body, you gambled with me,
Jules Bacon, Mr. America
Of 1943, not knowing it, asking me to bring
To the war's lost weight only
What I could do for myself, and just a little more
Each day, than I could do,

Seeking, among the heavy metals, those with the right
Heft for "this stage
Of my development," mý development,
Jules, as you said in the magazine, picking among
Scrap-iron   pig-iron   clutch-plates   armor-plate
Axles   train-track I could trade
For life, for new life.

Pig-iron giving its best
Would give it to me.   Scrap-iron, the iron
Of Stateside pigs, would give me *Strength*
And Health, would give me life,
Jules Bacon, survival.   Fitness
Rode in the crumpled fenders   the running-boards   the
    dashboards of jeeps
The upended motiveless axle
Of a six-by-six   parts of hydraulic systems
Tank-plates   armor-plate   coamings   cowl-flaps   ailerons
    rudders   light tanks
Gas-tanks of tanks   spent shells   shell-casings   .50 calibre casings
Sheets of armor-plate you were supposed to fold
Around you at twenty-thousand feet, against
The death-rust of ochre flak.

                I was looking for untested weight: anything
And everything that would bring out muscle

All over me, all sides
Of my face, Jules, except my jaws,
Which I would close
With bubble gum, and tighten to bring out
With Black Cow, muscles
My jaws didn't know they had,
Like Frankenstein, bolts hammered   smashed   bashed
Down through the jaws.

               My true self was everywhere lying and living
In swamps and sumps, gulleys and thickets,
Everywhere the war had thought of,
Lying with lizards in battery acid
Eaten with rain, in gulleys of weeds huddled   rusted   lying
Sideways all over the place.   Some still in crates, in cosmoline.
    Some still
Uncrated and rusting, not used
For anything.   What potential
For survival there was
In gulleys and Philippine canebrakes,
In miscellaneous casings and housings, floor-plates, clutch-plates.

               All I had to do was pick
By honest feel which weight was right; shape never mattered less,
And function never was in it.   Function
Changed in my hands.   Weight!   Weight!
And something I could get
My hands around.

            Clutch-pedals   boilers   boiler-plates
Pipe-lines   sewer-pipes: anything and everything with muscle
Part of it, could be made into muscle
All over me, beginning with where I stood,

Looking over the field of a battle already
Won and thrown away,
Or never used.

                My shoulders stood over the weeds
In light better than double suns.   My heart enlarged
Upward, for all of me, for I
Was ready to lift
          and you
Were with me, Jules Bacon, all the way, and would be
All the way home.

            In my mind, out over the weeds
Sickly with trash   with beggar-lice
Rust-paint   chipping paint   old paint

Even part of the track
Of a peace-time Filipino railroad,
Sections of track like jackstraw
Underfoot.   I wiped the sweat from my eyes.
The United States and the Philippines mixed
All over the ground, among the weeds
Piling higher than anyone's head, and I stood somewhere
Near the middle, hefting one thing
After the other, from sugar-mill fittings
To gun-mounts—however much I could put
Overhead while counting to ten with dead-bolt reckoning:
    refinery vats,
Ridge-pole of a sugar-mill,
Part of a cast-iron stove, part
Of a six-by-six axle   tongs   cam-shaft   drive-shaft
Crankshaft with hand-grips my country made
For me, Jules,

And you,
                part of a plow—what did they grow around here?
I had seen nothing but weeds, with radial
Engine-blocks in them, chopping
Mill-wheels   cable-wheels, the wheels
Ground-out for cables, the cables themselves
Coiled on green batteries—and just as I watched
A monitor lizard ran off, ran over,
Some kind of iguana standing in rain-
Water and battery fluid.
                    For you had said
That training is better
With supervision. But I had only mine, Jules, except
For your bell-tented image.
I wiped the wreck-sweat from my eyes
And selected
Carefully, and you with me bramble-bodied,
Worked through the weeds,
Jules Bacon, through the ankle-cuts
From weed-covered prongs
Of C-ration cans. You went with me
Weighing and choosing   rejecting. You were
With me from the beginning: picking   picking up
Part of a railroad track
To a sugar mill, thrown in with engine parts, and a hundred pounds
Better than gold. If you would preside,
Jules, I could mix the cultures.

                Railroad track: all right: I lifted it,

I curled it   I pressed it   I could do it
Barely: no YES I could do
Ten repetitions, and that made it ten times better

Than gold: it was right: *I* was right: we were right

For each other.   We were right on
The ball: wrecking ball ball bearings ball-sockets   ball-and-chain,
                    for you had said
In the magazine to work hard but not overdo
At first.   I was underdone,
Jules, but you stood in my tent on the cover
Of *Strength and Health,* Jules, with the build
I would die for, urging me all the time to build
Myself, not die: the body
That would save me from the war, the world-
Wreck I was in.

                 Standing over, overseeing
The wreckage, I brought it:
Carried it in wheel-barrows, in bags, in my hands
Burning hot from the weeds: a whole gym
Wrestled from lizards and assembled
Outside the tent, a selected scrap-heap
Of body-power gone pure with intent,
Intensity: a gym of my own, from the open sun-blasted dump
Of the military, the all-comers den of the used-up, unused
Parts of the war
With the build I wanted
To have come out
Of myself, the build of All-
America—in print you promised I could do it
If I would.   Nothing had anything to do
With luck: it was a matter of weight
And will: a body that would rise and live
Through the missions each night
Of each day that I worked

Out with the found heavy metals turned
Weightless and radiant, the throwaway tools
Of the war, part of a landing-mat strewn
With life, with my life
Somewhere in them,
And over them all, not like a bird,
Part of a swinging crane,
                      traded for muscle, Jules—
My muscle,
            among the monitor lizards,

Or some kind of lizard
Monitoring, ranging the war scrap.

                I would take my country's metals
Straight up from the Philippine Islands,
And raise them like exultation,
Like praise of you, Jules Bacon, Mr. America:
Would grip-down and raise up
And lift like a swinging crane
                the death-metals charged
With repetitions, swapping them for the best
I could buy of myself: new-living, new-veined muscle.

                Railroad track: I lifted it: I hefted it: I tried
To lift it: like lifting the whole heavy death yard.
I tried it on.   I lifted.   I tried it on myself,
My pectorals—or pecs as they were called
In *Strength and Health*—you called them,
Jules.

              It was what I could pick up,
And with it, could repeat

What you had said, could repeat
Myself ten times in a row, set by set,
Three days a week.

              I did the first ten for test
In the Park of Parts, in the hushed still-down
Of all available rust. The track was
The right track: I was right; we were right
For each other.   I hauled it freely
Then, down the dust road, a great lizard scrambling
From me without a name:
                          toted it
Past the top-heavy camions swaying
With boys, duty-bound for the flight-line: trucks
Swaying like limber groves with boys
I knew and didn't know:
                    the stubble-bearded bomber boys and day-fighters
Bound through sand for the flight line. But not I, Jules,
Until the night; not I, until that day
Turned dark.

              I rolled home the other way
By full sun in a wheelbarrow
To the tent, where you stood firm
Nailed to the center pole, and I could not fail
To understand and execute
Every movement
Of the clean-and-jerk, any phase of the military
Press: could not fail myself, and the weight itself
Would never fail.

             I pulled and bullied my gym
Loose from the war-junk, hauled and wheeled it to the living end

Of the dust road to the squadron
Area, to the tent,
                      straining to the gullet, heavily chewing
A whole pack of GI Spearmint for the pack
Of muscle at the sides
Of my jaws, and the hard-rock bars of chocolate
From Ten-in-One Rations, harder than Black Cow quarried
From grammar school, under
                Your tense friendly drop-forged smile.

            Web of veins
Distinctive as a finger-print
All over you: I wished to have mine
Emerge also and name me just there
And there and thére, and all
In one man, together,
            and real
At last, emerging, and stand there
As though some great thought
Thought me.   You were that mind,
Jules, there in the sun-dust,
Holding it all, with me
At the straining center slowly
Revealed, all powerful, proof
Against anything: against the ochre flak   against
Being lost   against the night sea, and especially
Against the air, unmoving, shining
With consequence: a wildfire of veins
Re-written now all over myself
Like a new self-born life,
Branching as I strained in place to lift
And live: hand-holds as though government-made
For me exactly.

                    Nobody thought
Anything about it, Jules; everybody in the squadron was insane
With survival schemes.   Everyone had his own
Life-time guarantee
For life   for survival, practiced
Some in secret, like a vice, a truth too big
To believe, for going home better than he shipped out:
Making rings from Australian coins,
Flying kites, playing softball
Or volleyball, studying
Math or civil engineering,
Learning Greek, or reading back through the lieutenants
Of Robert E. Lee.
                    In broad daylight I had mine,
With you
Watching from the belled shadows outward through the blind sunlight
Where I worked out,
Jules Bacon, winner of the first time chosen things
Other than measurements, or bulk
Or symmetry, but also for teeth   hair
Complexion   agility   grace: for "overall
pleasingness of aspect."
                    Grace I could not get to.   Lost hair, lost teeth
I would have to find
Some way to make up for,
But with the axle-tree, with the sugar-track
I went for bulk: for inches
On the arm, on the thighs, on the pectorals and trapezius,
More everything
I didn't have, everything
I needed to raise on me
And above me, and I knew I must go

With the track, with the crankshaft,
With the boiler-plate all the way
For inches, pounds
And inches, for bulk, and maybe
Symmetry would come, and maybe even teeth
And hair come back.

                But inches: but pounds:
If I could get these, I believed, they would get me through
The night missions, in one
Piece, Jules, in one
New piece.

                    It would be better than coming back
From the dead: far more impressive, physically,
Than Lazarus.
               I could go toward you where the track
Broke off in my hands, rising
Above the weeds and the junk,
When I would disassemble
The black cosmolined parts of the aircraft,
Pull the railroad track from the lizards and weeds
And muscle it up,
                    and flying would then be
Like re-assembling the black-backed aircraft and building it
    around me
As a new form of life, not reachable
By any orange flak over Tay Tay.

               You gave me that, Jules Bacon, from your pole
Where you were slant
And posted, in the hot dark
With the centipedes and day-rats, steaming

In shadow, shining with muscle, smiling
Outward on me where I worked
In the open sun for my life
With railroad track in my hands
To become me, to be something
Better than me, but me.
The floor-boards of the tent
Not metal   not stone: wood rotting
That was fairly new wood
Before the rains: ammo boxes, crate-slats, barrels, parts of nail-kegs,
Boxes bashed to pieces when they'd been emptied
Into the sky, pine-planks, laths, duck-boards:
                        new wood, day before yesterday.
There you stood, Jules,
In rain and sun with me,
Two rainy seasons in New Guinea
Carried through flood-stage rivers   through storms where it
    rained
Rats   centipedes   malaria   elephantiasis: packed carefully exactly
In the middle of my A-3 bag:
Shoes   boots   socks and shorts
On the bag-floor and, above, the sheep-
Lined heavy leather of flight:
                        around and above you, around
Your herdsman's unfaked smile,
Packed deep in there
Away from the enemy's weathers: safe   safe
From the strafing run   from the enemy   from everything:
Your smooth, bunched
But unbloated muscles, your centaur's calf
With the bullet-hole from some civilian
Accident. You were out of the rain, Jules,
And in the center

Of the war to do the most good
For whomever beheld you: unmoved mover
Of heavy rusty track, of a whole junk-yard: a whole depot.

                         For leg-lifts, all-out
Weight, as much as I could get up
With everything I had,
And a little more. Squats: the weight-lifter's demonic "crash":
           "All you've got,
Till the weight won't move. Just won't." I would

Bear-up like an axle, squatting, with as much
As an axle would bear with me
Under it, wheels rusting
Overhead, unspinning. I couldn't "get it up"
Was not what I meant; we could all do that: I meant

Weight   weight for me   the exact weight and number
Of repetitions
For survival, squatting with as much
As I could get up, then finishing off
With two matched cylinder-casings, light
Weight   many repetitions,
Jules, for "definition,"
As you said: cast-iron casings   cylinders pitted
With monsoons   corroded   eroded,
But the same weight
As each other, or nearly.

                         There, under the hot roasting sack
Of the tent, your body shining with linseed
And Three-In-One oil,
I set them, turned orange-black with work and sun

And atabrine, with two rainy seasons in New Guinea,
Carried through storms   flood-stage rains

Staging areas   transient camps, packed in the exact
Lost middle of my A-3 bag, boots and socks below you
On the bag-floor, thick-handed gloves
Above: leather jackets, dingy-wooled sheep-pants
Clipped from the sad clouds
Of combat-flight, packed deep in there with the sheep-boots,
Out of the war, out of the rains
Of Nadzah, holding your winning pose, grinning
With grease and shining
With "perfect symmetry": your bracketed muscles pleasing enough
To keep me alive through the night
Of the dark engines, my own
And the enemy's, through the orange-blunting flak,
In cut-off Class A's,

      for I
Had lifted the bombed-out sugar-track
From the ashes, the weeds and the lizards, my hands burning
With rust and wild hope
That my overhead quivering sustained.
The wobbling crankshaft would get me there, bring me
With the other boys riding
On their secret disciplines, home,

Jules, if I could do it:
Could repeat   repeat myself
Enough times to change   really
To change and stay in the world
With the tottering crankshaft and raise
     and raise   and repeat   and raise

Overhead the bombed melt-down of track:
                              raise   raise and repeat the rising
Of the sugar-track.

Alternate leg-lifts   for back-work, Jules, you said.
Alternate   alternate   alternate
                     with plenty of weight.
Few repetitions   crash   crash   all you can do
This time   all   ALL
You can do.   All I had
Was the axle and the track.
By taking on the work-load
Of presses and curls, classic and reverse, I could bring
The raising of the sugar-track
Into my arms.

Looking in on you
With the sun dust-blocked full on me,
I set my shoulders
To change what I would have to be, to live.

                     You manned me,
Jules Bacon, outside
The tent where I stood in a fiery wonderment
Of new veins, emerging all over me
Not for my country or for danger
At twenty-thousand feet, but for what I would be
On peaceful home ground, finding myself inside
The wild blue veins of excess all alone,
But not, Jules, all alone
For me,
And not in the belled interior.

You stood alone with linseed oil
And Three-in-One, your heroic abdominals
In the photograph growing tighter,
Tighter and brighter as you stood,
Your smile, though friendly,
Tight-strung as racquet-gut,
Eye-levelling with me.
                    You gave me eye-to-eye power,
From where you stood in the tent, staring
With all your stark veins
Out into the sand-bagged sun, out of the tilted dark,
Far from remembering the rains
Of Dulag, Jules Bacon, smiling and peeling, tattering
Away, Jules, in the combat tropics.

                    After the last inverted curl   the last
Military press   the last pump,
The body I was slaving for would rise
In the night air,
Dark on dark, but shining
Black with the held sun: would rise and ride,

With no fear, on the principle of life
Itself, through the blanking
Orange flak of Palawan   Jojo Island   Sanga Sanga
Where Jack Blake died last week, and Jason MacGiffin
The week before, the roaming blunderbussing
Beast-hunt of flak, glowing with more
Than the sun.

                    Held-in by body-work, held together
To "fly and fight," shining with foundry-heat
And form, my body tight

And bright all over me, radiant
With the last pump, with my earnest
And mystical sweat,
                        and even if the enemy
Loved me, I would not fail—and could see me
Not fail—would have to suffer
From the last donkey-lift, the last curl, the last military
Press: something alive and continuing
Through the blanking, bashing wilderness of flak
Over Formosa,

                  heaving the weight straight up
From Base: straight up and out
Of the heart, one eye-shut repetition
More.   Listen, I worked there
For life.   The hotter the tent got,
Building the stench of its canvas,
Jules, simmering
Around you, the harder I worked
In the all-out sun, and then went in, facing
Your proud friendly centaur-calved shadow
And lay in all-out sweat on the cot, pulsing
With exultation, perfect in the ochre dust

Of Mindoro, where I had pulled and bullied
My gym loose from the war-junk, over the last piece
Of track of the bombed-out sugar-mill,
The railroad rising back
Into its life in my arms, out of the weeds,
Above the barren-egged lizards, like raising all
The undestroyed track to Calapan,
                        and then my arms tight
With the last pump and a micro-

Millimeter rounder. I would go in to you
Where you stood nailed
To the tent-pole, some kind of prayer
Involved, where the muscles alone,
And not the heart, did the praying. It was pure life,
Jules, muscle-fire, my weight-work
And dust-excited mind come in
And find, in what I had done,
What I could do
And be, life lengthening in my muscles
Past the war.

                    I would let fall
The axle-tree   the railroad
Track, and go in
And in, out of the sun, and like wildfire stand
With you, Jules: stand with you for a moment,
Just as it was: pure veins and muscles,
And in it a heart
Beating like cables
In wind: a new man
Outlined from a boy in full inaugural
Wildfire blood now visible
In blue all over me where I had worked
In the enemy's sun, lifted
Into relief, stamped endlessly by the numbers
Into the body I was slaving for.
I would rise in the dark air   lofted   enspirited,
Exultant, boiling and pouring my juices, shining
In the dark from sun-work,
                            sweating
Down to the first and last definition, the slowly-found
Essential, my breath coming

Like broom-straw until even the veins
In my gut began to stand
For themselves.

I would shave my chest and legs,
The day peace was declared, and slather myself
Not with linseed oil, Jules,
Like you, but with cosmoline, a tribute
To the metal that had made me, and oil myself
Like superhuman metal, fully inhuman
At last: all body,
Not needing a soul, beginning to stand
Forth like a new man,
                          For I had trapped
The enemy's sun in its sleep, something
I could do
Down to the soaring veins, something
I could reach with my blood, and make it
Branch in new veins:
A new man I did not know
But had made and charged
With my new blood, bright with the last pump,
That had been mine all the time,

                        when I laddered myself
High into the black aircraft, re-tightened as though singing
With set-screws, with plumb-line certainty,
Locked-in, locked-on,
Inspired, sex-strong
With exercise, with over-work
And sun from the military
Junk-yard, Jules, from dead-end odds
And ends,

                    the bucket-seat
Alive as a pressing bench
Haloed with axle-rust.   I came into the place
Of my power, as the aircraft pulsed
With what I had
Been doing in your shadow.

Advance, Jules.   Come to, come over me
From the tent-pole,
With your dim indispensible help,
With new muscle from your nailed shadow.
The engines roared
With survival: with trees,
With children, with death
To the enemy's children,
But not to me, Jules Bacon,
                for my pecs, triceps, lats, abdominals and all,
And all I was getting,
I was getting from you,
From Mr. America
Himself.   Like you, I believed
I could have it all, though I could not
Fool myself: I had it all
But the good teeth, Jules: teeth, hair, and grace
I did not have, and could not get
Though I would have tried: tried anything
Under your shadow,   though I had teeth—most—
And some hair, and all,
All but grace.   But what I had, Jules, came from the reclaimed axle,
From the hand-held railroad track,
The fragment of heavy transport
Transporting me: track I now felt I could
Have broken off by hand.

                  For the next day,
After the flak I would clamp
Down on my Black Cow and lift
And live, sleeves rolling over
My biceps and new Class-A's cut-off, and now
No shirt, no shorts toward the end,
Only a jock-strap
Against the hernias, as you said,
In your sweat
Of survival.

                  I would fly on, held together
By repetitions, by the molar-baring talley of weight, chewing
Spearmint or Black Cow, hissing,
Hoisting, running on air,
On strain, on enemy sunlight.

                  Then seated tightly in the bucket
Seat, in the webbed glow of harness glowing
like hometown Atlanta, the last all-out push
Or pull, each work-stunned muscle bright,
Glowing like set-screws.   Each tendon leapt, potent beyond
Not death, but being killed,
Leapt past the blueprints
Straight into the engines, and remade them,
Into the trembling unthinkable
Idea of the engines.
                              The working sun was down,
Jules, and black was the color
Of new life. The dead engines caught
Like bracketing fire and I rose
Over you, and with you, out of your silent

Bright image:
I roared, you roared, the engines roared,
                              the good sweat shining
Like linseed, like cosmoline under my overalls,
The fabric-drench of energy earned by glory-sweat
Of overwork, dense as the sweat
Of metal. Like Three-In-One pulled together,
The engines pulled, drew into parallel, tightened,
Surged the length and true beasthood
Of the aircraft, everything shuddering
With continuance, confident with survival
As the whole body caught, stood on its locked wheels.

                    I have shot my arms,
I tell you, straight past the biceps,
With a railroad in them,
Past the sawed ragged edge of my flight suit: nothing
Was separate: everything was jacketed
Together, shining like linseed
And cosmoline, the propellers luminous
With harmony,

Not junk, but now a whole machine
To which I had mastery
In my muscles, Jules, do you hear. Pistons
Took fire from my left hand, from my body
And body to come: spoke together, matched, paralleling
Like the engines, timed
For it. I trundled out of the grave
Of the revetment, lumbered out "to fly
And fight," glowing with health
And muscles and ego,
Alive and alert in the timelessness

Of take-off, the engines agonizing
In the grip and shake of full hold-back,
Shuddering like dogs.   My left hand thrust
Forward, the engines leapt in labor-heavy joy,
Broke ground and took on
The luminous weave of the mat-strip, myself gone
Luminous as the riding-lights,
Alive all the way down
The whole runway, slamming and slanting with runway-power,
Rising full into the unequal air
Through searchlights, the ochre of flak,
Into one long battering light: I broke

Entirely from earth.   This was it.   This was the whole thing
We could do against death.
Vital with waiting in the great grave
Of the revetment, the aircraft leapt the exact length
And breadth it was born for, Jules.
The props caught the whole air
Where it lived.   Metal and muscle fused
Like a new natural element
Whose heart was joy: alive, on fire
With each other, glowing and tight
With identity.
                    The runway opened
Slowly, with all its speed came forward
With the throttle, pouring
Into my mouth, Jules,
With no end to it, no end but life.   Life!
War roared with life, and you saved me.

James Dickey's Intention

An Afterword to *Death, and the Day's Light*

By Dave Smith

During my college years poetry was little more than a subdivision of literature to me, here and there modestly compelling, something my fellow students delighted in "unpacking," as we say now, but a form of speech I didn't quite get. But when I read James Dickey's "May Day Sermon to the Women of Gilmer County, Georgia, by a Woman Preacher Leaving the Baptist Church," which appeared in *The Atlantic Monthly* in the summer of 1965, I got it. I felt, as the evangelists proclaim, washed in the blood, transformed, and it is not exaggeration to say my life was changed, my path set, whatever passed for an interior consciousness in me shaken toward the view Robert Penn Warren, typically sardonic, assayed in half a line: "so this is the world!"

Part of my experience with Dickey was, as I became a small magazine editor, to plead to publish any of his poems. He was very generous. In 1968 I published his poem "The Wheelchair Drunk" in a tiny college journal. My naiveté prevented me from knowing he was extremely provident with his poems, publishing far fewer than many colleagues, placing them in prestigious venues, selling them—imagine!—instead of giving them away. In the 1990s, as co-editor of *The Southern Review*, I asked again. Dickey had shifted some of his energies to fiction, but I believed, correctly, he had continued to write poems, for I had seen the occasional one appear. He permitted me to publish "Last Hours," a wonderful poem, sure to make its way in a late collection. That collection never came about.

In the spring of 1997, the news came that James Dickey had died. I had driven up from Baton Rouge to visit a few months earlier, encountering a skeleton of the voracious lion I had met only a handful of times, the shadow of the end clear enough. Still, his death was stunning, not quite believable. Yea or nay, it was Big Jim. How could he be taken? Soon it seemed to me that every piece of correspondence I had from writers took the occasion to provide an anecdote, some brief and some not so brief, all colorful and not a few in some respect seeming scarred by an old encounter with the poet whose presence could not be ignored nor acknowledged only. It had to be *narrated*. Even for those who had not actually known James Dickey, he was felt character in the way William James spoke of a "felt fact." How common it was then to greet a fellow poet, especially southern variants, with words one fumbled over trying to register the absence of this looming, loquacious, and in every way large man. I remember saying, "his death leaves a hole in the landscape," and then trying to describe what I meant until the effort trailed off into some other subject. Death leaves our mouths full of nothing, words jamming up in place of meaning—but not eloquent with meaning. That is for writing.

Randall Jarrell, a poet Dickey had much admired, tried to capture the unsayable feeling we have when death has come to a human figure we struggle to fit into our usual idiom. Writing in "Say Goodbye to Big Daddy" of the professional football player Big Daddy Lipscomb, who had the kind of size and presence in his world that Dickey had in southern letters, Lipscomb having been a defensive tackle for the Baltimore Colts and much reputed for his violent, aggressive play, Jarrell's poem noted the ferocious Lipscomb couldn't sleep for fears that bedeviled him, so much so that death came as a release. At least it appeared so to Jarrell, who wrote in the penultimate line, "The world won't be the same without Big Daddy." It is the mouthful of praise we stop with, all we can muster, often repeated at services for the deceased, at best a partial truth. But Jarrell, and James Dickey would have admired this especially, couldn't tolerate anything less than whole truth, and raw truth, so he pushed his poem one stinging line further, writing, "or else it will be."

Seventeen years after Dickey's death, Jarrell's contradictory sentiments are both correct: nothing is the same in poetry as it was while Dickey was writing and publishing. And yet poets live, they come to prominence, they fade, they die. The world moves on, relentlessly, and today even graduate students in American poetry must be introduced to Dickey's poems that for decades dominated and filled the pages of *The Atlantic* and *The New Yorker* and *Poetry* and every journal of respect in the academy. It will serve no purpose here to argue how regrettable is this ignorance of a body of literary accomplishment, this ultimate dismissal of the most intense human effort to make experience both present and timeless, for surely we know there are no poets, have been none and will be none who do not suffer the diminution of being forgotten. It scarcely matters what greatness to which they rise. Forgotten. Not absolutely, of course, but in such that slide, as in nearness to the mortal end, degrees count.

Dickey believed, or so I think anyway, that nothing good and great could be forgotten, not for long, but rather it would rise up like the flood-buried parts of Appalachian villages in his famous 1970 novel *Deliverance*. It may be the perilous and fragile life of the poet, whose end constantly lies before him, requires that he believe in a kind of rediscovery that is itself a reincarnation, about which Dickey wrote finely, and that may explain why Milton and Frost, among so many masters, worried in words about "fame." At any rate, Dickey's conviction that his poetry would last, however it might fade and then return, was bedrock. That supported his determination to write to his own interior standard of quality, to perform as it were what *his* imagination alone accessed. The language of poetry is mostly ordinary machinery to readers but, to the true poet, it can become a superior language, full of more, and worth more, and thus in the poet's hands it can be challenged, tutored, shaped, trained, pushed to a place that is, well, *beyond*.

When he yet remained famous, and no portrait of the poet as a socio-literary phenomenon better depicts such delirious fame than Dickey's self-portrait in "Barnstorming for Poetry," collected in *Babel to Byzantium*, when he was yet a prime subject of the critical industry, Dickey's life in poetry soared like the stock market with brilliance, accomplishment, and bravado. But the big show turned to a slow and late decline into what many viewed as poems of dithering opacity. The later poems included in *The Whole Motion: Collected Poems*, poems of the 80s and 90s, baffled even partisan readers, his motion seeming perversely slowed, defiantly contemplative for a poet whose modus operandi was action. Doubtless some of the public response came of generational difference; some was due to historical distance—World War II's personal violations and obligations, primary subjects to veterans like Dickey, felt more than remote to undergraduates drifting from their parents' lives to Hippy revolution. But even the far-outest visionaries would land among the library dust where today dissertations and academic monographs, in one way or another, tell a common story of what has happened to those known as the Contemporary American Poets in anthologies by Donald Hall, Mark Strand, A.L. Poulin and others.

William Stafford, Louis Simpson, Carolyn Kizer, Richard Hugo, luminous James Wright—all no longer shine in the poetic nights. James Dickey, perhaps the most incandescent in orbit, like Whitman's Lincoln drooped in the darkness. Why? The plainest argument, among the most frequently offered in various forms, was one that Paul Ramsey, a fellow southerner and poet, of somewhat lesser quality and accomplishment, proposed. Dickey, Ramsey wrote, had early found a splendidly fecund and appropriate language for poetry but, like the undisciplined son, abandoned it for a lesser, if more glamorous, tongue. Dickey, who liked to give interviews in which he measured his shop-work against peers, made very clear what he was doing was at every point deliberate; his intention was *change* from the old way of a poem's business, change to his own habits and practices, change as the god's way to potential vision, great treasure, new worlds. It was very American, but not conservative, and not pietistic American. It was hold on and go for it. Well, you get little points in literature for good intention, though it might be argued the value in Allen Ginsberg and in Robert Bly lies in what their intentions wrought in the poetic zeitgeist more than in poems they wrought.

Whatever the changes he rang, Dickey valued more than any poet I have ever read the possibility of *excitement*. In MFA programs much is taught of rules, histories, imitations, the mastery of the heritage of poetry, and that is entirely proper for schooling. But great teaching has an obligation to identify the nature and character of great poems, and I do not believe it can be denied the experience of this character, often called joy, is fundamentally to excite the reader. In forty years of teaching in this industry, I have never witnessed one poet encourage a student to strive to make the poem exciting. Dickey did it constantly. That was what I encountered when I read the "May Day Sermon." One had only to hear James Dickey read a poem once, his or any poem he admired, and it was nakedly evident poems could be exciting, could be different, and suddenly the issue of change, in so many respects, stood central with each who heard him—even if he or she couldn't say that. Exactly. Because it was central to Dickey, always, and viscerally. Change, and God knows the southern writers thrive on that subject, is a devil, a burden, a curse. What pastoralist doesn't feel that? But change for Dickey was the great good, everything, the edge to get out on, the place of discovery, where life mattered most, and where more crucially than in poems? If you want to understand Dickey, think of the men and canoes toppling under whitewater in *Deliverance*, the same scene done well enough as a southern Gothic set-piece in his earlier poem "On the Coosawattee," the instant of buoyant pulse and surge repeated again and again in his poetry as he found and re-found that secret under-current that continually changes everything.

Dickey never stopped pursuing a change-up, a change off, whatever surprised him and nudged his imagination forward. It is in that sense, I believe, the late poems have been utterly undervalued, misread, viewed as a veering off into a dead-end rather than an evolving rhythm, especially the most startling work he did in his dying years on the poems Gordon Van Ness has edited as *Death, and the Day's Light*. Van Ness, in a very helpful introduction, argues the five shorter lyrics Dickey collected here—"Conch," "The Drift-Spell," "Last Hours," "The Confederate Line at Ogeechee Creek," and "Entering Scott's Night"—manifest recognizable kinship with all of his poetic concerns and subjects. Oblique and ritually prophetic at moments, intimate speech to his brother at moments, their style veers from private meditation to public oratory, conflating and confusing signals to readers, tonally mitigating directions and over-correcting, not unlike a barnstorming pilot. But for all its lacunae and dis-locution, Dickey's late poetry nevertheless has, as patient readers will recognize, the signature of Dickey's cosmic grappling, the phrase-making no man in his time makes more memorably. To see this evolution, I recommend the towering and complete collection of the omnibus Dickey, edited by Ward Briggs, *The Complete Poems of James Dickey* (U of South Carolina Press, 2013), but *Death, and the Day's Light*, the posthumous and final volume by Dickey, completes and confirms the trajectory of this poet's work. If he risks lapsing into faux-visionary crooning, Dickey's oracular male voice continues trying to connect not only what consciousness encounters but also what it intuits. To me, the short poems are delightful assurances the old man had plenty of juice when we so often mourned his dithering. But there is this other as well.

Dickey had been working on what he called "Two Poems on the Survival of the Male Body." He, like Robert Penn Warren, developed a penchant for doing poems in linked structures, in pairs, sequences, and suites, each part given its sub-division name. The first of the "Two Poems," virtually a book-length work by itself, is called "Show Us the Sea." A colloquy in which Dickey's son is the silent auditor, and a kind of ritual chant mounted to provoke the elements to stand and display, the poem lacks manifest drama that structures, its meandering a form experiment that wants less to describe the sea and its enduring-ness than to become the language of what is beyond that enduring-ness, and communicate it to the son who will survive. It is about what being a father of a son means, trying to say that meaning, knowing the sea itself knows and says it continuously. This is the old ground and the old work of Dickey's best known poems, but his scope, his canvas, his struggle is, if not grander, so much bigger.

The second half of the "Two Poems" is a kind of super-elegy. "For Jules Bacon" cites and whirls around the life of a body-builder who became a legendary model for American GIs during World War II. I suspect all America males at some life-stage imagine themselves stronger, muscled-up, and make desultory efforts to entice "the body." Then we move on. Some, though, concentrate better, work harder, becoming a "body-builder" whose bulked-up physique implies superior ability to resist and to discipline life's randomness. Such builders spend themselves in becoming themselves, literally exercising themselves into and through the language of pain in order to self-create, for they want to be something we have only imagined and something that will cease as soon as the intensity of becoming desists. In the weirdness and anxiety of World War II, young American boys not only wanted a beach body, they also needed all the help they could give themselves because each life stood vulnerable in every moment. Jules Bacon, a serene model of prowess, sculpted and fearless, showed up on magazine covers that showed up in bivouac tents in Pacific combat areas. Poetry might help bear life, but Jules Bacon also showed what you needed to knock out the enemy.

Is it contradictory to think building the body so that it has a chance to manage change is analogous to building the language toward the chance of truth?

I know of little in American poetry like what Dickey does in *Death, and the Day's Light*, but much in "For Jules Bacon" will be familiar in its way. Dickey liked to make poems from the point of "what if"—less inclined to attend to a past than to lean forward. His narrator finds himself among the cast-off debris of war surplus materials, a kind of junkyard in which the soldiers and airmen live while the war churns around them. Much of the poem chronicles that stuff. It leads to the rhythmic repeating common to Dickey's drafts (as anyone who examines his work in special collections will see). Dickey was an over-writer, a duplicator of lines and phrases to which he slowly added or subtracted until the final poem was edited, cut, sewn, smoothed, seamed, precisely orchestrated—something Van Ness has done his best to approximate, a form of "helping" Dickey finish an unfinished poem. On the whole, I believe the publication of *Death, and the Day's Light* is a welcome event, one for whom we owe a debt of gratitude to Gordon Van Ness, whose light-handedness in his task seems admirable and honorable There will be disagreement about his process and its results. Some delight to see a poem's innards still visible; some gag at that. No doubt the bottom feeders still among us will hold, Thus have the mighty fallen, and ain't it a good day after all. Well no, and yes.

Still, Van Ness does not claim *Death, and the Day's Light* stands with Dickey's best, and he is cautious about how we should understand this prodigal appearance, gently and properly so. Though I am uncertain an "afterword" is the place to do it, I feel compelled to ask why Dickey chose to spend his last energies on body-building, male models, the oil-and-tan life of mirror dwellers, a matter so exotic that even for this cultivator of the richly bizarre it holds an almost inexplicable whiff. Well, that was Dickey, wasn't it—the poem as the entrance to the unmade, a wiggle into interior experience as the idiom of exterior expression. Let us say one explanation may be altogether simple. Play. Gaming. The pursuit of excitement in competition. Dickey kept writerly journals in which, as in his interviews, he liked to observe his working self, his subjects and potentials. One often finds him asking, "what can be done with this?" It is the query of a working man, a man in whom the spirit of creation swells. The answer, often silent but never absent, is to make a better self. Imagine it, dramatize it, see what it can do. Our imaginations have been at work inventing superior selves as far back as we care to look—at the task of creating super-heroes, then having to consider what the ethical obligations of such as Superman and Spiderman and Milton's Satan may be. Taking that view of characters, and sending them hurtling off in our innermost dramas—as my four grandsons are doing this weekend with their Lego-brigades—leads even to theosophy and philosophy. If a poet is any good, and Dickey was—is—awfully good, one can see that goodness trying to work out the knots and niches and thorny ways where life is random and in tension. Poems are acts of what we intend, or intended, for our selves. They begin with the parts, disconnected and lying about and in need of a creating spirit, as Dickey says:

> All junk there is
> Consists of whole parts, and this holds: holds true and creates
> In wars, great dumps and yards,
> Fields and sumps, swamps

and, with what we find, we build what we can be:

> I was looking for untested weight: anything
> And everything that would bring out muscle
> All over me, all sides

and if we are lucky, and good, the experience may be thrilling and redemptive. Dickey seemed to think that was worth taking into a poem, letting it lead him where he could go with it, from Jules Bacon, cover star and Mr. America of 1943, even in the death-days of Pacific war, to something every man needs. Maybe especially then. Dickey wrote, "War roared with life, and you saved me." Perhaps James Dickey, in a life of vitalizing poetry, has done his share of saving. Anyway, his intention was to discover and enact the excitement of play that creates. As he might have said, the "in-creation" that going is, especially if it leads *beyond more*.

Index

Aleixandre, Vicente xx
Alnilam xv, xx
Anabasis xxviii
"Apollo" xxi
Apostrophe xv
Aristotle xxiii, xxv
Atlanta magazine xv
Babel to Byzantium 82
Bacon, Jules xxviii, 85, 87
Barbour, Wendell xiii
"Barnstorming for Poetry" 82
Barnouw, A. J. xx
Baughman, Judy xii
Beddoes, Thomas Lovell ix, xxxiv
Belitt, Ben xxiv
Benfield, Rob xxvi
Biespel, David xxv
Big Daddy Lipscomb 80
Bigham, Bill xxvi
Blake, William xxiii
Bly, Robert xxv, 83
Bottoms, David xiii
Bradley, Mrs. Earl xii
Briggs, Ward xi, xii, xxxv, xxxvi, 84
Buckdancer's Choice xix, xxiv
Bundy, Ted xxx
Calhoun, Richard xx, xxii
Carter, Jimmy xxi
Chappell, Fred xxiii
"Circuit" xxvii
Coen Brothers xv
"Conch" xiii, xiv, xv, xxxiii, xxxiv, 84
Crux xv
"Daughter" xxviii
Davison, Peter xx
"De Dierenriem" xx
Deliverance xi, xix, xx, xxvi, 81, 83

"Diabetes" xix, xxv
Dickey, Bronwen x, xii, xvi, xxviii
Dickey, Christopher ix, xii, xvi
Dickey, Deborah (Dodson) xii, xxii, xxvi, xxxi
Dickey, Kevin x, xii, xvi, xxvi, xxvii, 84
Dickey, Maibelle xxvi
Dickey, Maxine xix, xxvi, xxvii
Dickey, Tom xxix, xxx, xxxi
Dick Goodwin Trio xxxi
"Double-tongue: Collaborations and Rewrites" xxiv
Douglas, William xxi
"Dover: Believing in Kings" xxvii
"Drifting" xxxv
"Drinking from a Helmet" xviii, xxxv
Drowning with Others xvii, xviii
Emory University x, xii, xv, xxxiii, xxxvi
"Entering Scott's Night" xii, xiii, xxx, xxxi, xxxiii, 84
Fairman, Carol xii, xv
"Falling" xxv
Fitzgerald, F. Scott xxxi
Five Points xxxiii
"Fog Envelops the Animals" xvii
"For Jules Bacon" xiii, xiv, xv, xvi, xxv, xxvi, xxviii, xxix, xxx, xxxi-xxxii, xxxiii, xxxiv, xxxv, xxxvi, 85
"For the Death of Lombardi" xxi
Franklin, Ben xv
Frost, Robert xxxvi, 81
Ginsberg, Allen xxiii, 83
"Giving a Son to the Sea" xxvi, xxvii
God's Images xxi

Greiner, Don xii, xv
Guthrie, Tim xii, xxvi
Gwynn, R. S. xxi
Hall, Donald 82
Harper's Weekly xxx
Hart, Henry xii, xxiv
Haupt, Jonathan xiii
Havird, David xxiv
"Head-Deep in Strange Sounds" xx
Helmets xvii, xviii
"Hero" xiv
Heylen, Romy xxiv
Hill, Robert xx, xxii
Hölderlin, Friedrich ix
Hugo, Richard 82
In Pursuit of the Grey Soul xxi
Into the Stone xvi, xvii, xviii, xix, xxv, xxxiv
James Dickey at 70 xv
James Dickey Newsletter xii
James, William xvii, 80
Jericho: The South Beheld xxi
Jarrell, Randall 80
Jolley, Marc xi, xiii
Keesey, Doug xviii
Kizer, Carolyn 82
"Knock" xix
"Last Hours" xiii, xxx, xxxi, xxxiii, 79, 84
Lensing, George xxi
"Listening to Foxhounds" xvii
Lombardi, Vince xxi
Longwood University xiii
Lowell, Robert xxi, xxv
"Madness" xix
March of the Ten Thousand xxviii
Marsman, Hendrick xx
"May Day Sermon" 79, 83

Melville, Herman xx
Mercer University Press xi, xiii
"Mercy" xix
"Messages" xxvi
"Metaphor as Pure Adventure" xxiii
Milton, John 81, 87
Mitgang, Herbert xxiii
Moby-Dick xx
Montale, Eugenio xx
National Book Award xix, xxiv
Newsweek xvi
"On the Coosawattee" xviii, 83
"On the Hill Below the Lighthouse" xxvii
On the Survival of the Male Body xiv, xv
Pair, Joyce xii
Partisan Review xiv, xxxiv
Paz, Octavio xx
Penn Warren, Robert xx, 79, 84
"Pier Bowling Alley" xiv
"Pine" xviii, xxxv
Plato xxiii
Poems 1957–1967 xxi
Poetry 81
Poulin, A. L. 82
Pound, Ezra xxiv
Princeton University Library Chronicle xv
Puella xix, xxi, xxii
Ramsey, Paul 82
"Reading *Genesis* to a Blind Child" xxvii
"Reluctance" xxxvi
Richards, Meg xii, xv
"Sand-Aging" xiv
Satan 87
"Say Goodbye to Big Daddy" 80
Seamster, Lisa xiii

Self-Interviews xvii
Sexton, Anne xxiii
Sherman, Gen. William Tecumseh xxx
Shoemaker, Kathy xii
"Show Us the Sea" ix, xiii, xiv, xv, xvi, xxv, xxvi, xxvii, xxviii, xxx, xxxi-xxxii, xxxiii, xxxiv, xxxv, xxxvi, 84
Silverstein, Norman xxii
Simpson, Louis 82
Smith, Dave xiii
Sorties xix
Spiderman 87
Stafford, William 82
"Stopping by Woods on a Snowy Evening" xxxvi
Strand, Mark 82
Strength and Health xxix
Striking In xxxvii
Suarez, Ernest xii
Superman 87
The Atlantic Monthly 79, 81
"The Bee" xxv, xxvii
"The Being" xxxv
"The Cancer Match" xix, xxv
The Central Motion xviii, xxiv
"The Common Grave" xxxv
The Complete Poems of James Dickey xi, xiii, xxxv, 84
"The Confederate Line at Ogeechee Creek" xii, xiii, xxx, xxxi, xxxii, 84
"The Drift-Spell" xiii, xiv, xv, xxxiii, 84
"The Driver" xvii
"The Eagle's Mile" xxi
The Eagle's Mile xxi, xxii, xxiii, xxiv
The Early Motion xviii

The Enemy from Eden xxi
"The Energized Man" xix
"The Escape" xxvii
The Eye-Beaters, Blood, Victory, Madness, Buckhead and Mercy xix
"The Firebombing" xxix
"The Leap" xx
"The Lifeguard" xvii, xxvii
"The Little More" xxxv
"The Movement of Fish" xxvii
The New Yorker xv, xxxi, xxxiii, 81
The New York Times xxiii
"The One" xxvii
The One Voice of James Dickey x
"The Other" xxix
The Owl King xxi
The Oxford Quarterly Review xiv, xv
"The Performance" xxv
"The Scarred Girl" xxv
"The Signs" xxvii
The Southern Review xxxiii, 79
"The Strength of Fields" xxi
The Strength of Fields xix, xx, xxi
"The Three" xxvii
"The Wheelchair Drunk" 79
The Whole Motion xiv, xix, xxv, xxxv, 82
The Zodiac xviii, xix, xx, xxi, xxii, xxiv, xxxv
"To His Children in Darkness" xxvii
"Tomb Stone" xxvii
To the White Sea xv, xxviii
"Turning Away" xxxv
"Two Poems on the Survival of the Male Body" ix, xiv, xv, xxxiv, xxxvi, 84, 85

"Two Poems: Son and His Mother" xv, xxxiii
University of South Carolina xii, xv, xxxi, xxxiii
University of South Carolina Press xiii, 84
Van Ness, Gordon x, xi, xvi, xxxv, 84, 86
"Venom" xix
Washington and Lee College xxvi
Washington Post Book World xxv
Washington University xxxvi
"Wave and Slack Return" xiv-xv
Wayfarer xxi
Wesleyan University Press xix
Whitman, Walt xxi, xxviii, 82
Winters, Yvor xxiii
Wright, James 82
Xenophon xxviii